Creating Wealth
In Declining
Real Estate Markets

How to **Get Rich** in The Best
Real Estate Investment Market
In 50 Years or More!

by Don Loyd

Don Loyd

ISBN: 9781460935590
1460935594

Printed in America

Second Printing

10 9 8 7 6 5 4 3 2

Disclaimer

This book is sold with the understanding that the author and publisher are not engaged in rendering legal, accounting, or other professional services. Every effort has been made to make this book as complete and accurate as possible. However, since humans are fallible, there may be mistakes, both typographical and in content. Therefore, this book should be used only as a general guide and not as the ultimate source if the information contained herein. The author and publisher shall not be liable or responsible to any person or entity with respect to any loss or damage caused, or alleged to have been caused, directly or indirectly, by the information contained in this book,

Published by
DreamMaker Press
Denver, CO

Acknowledgements

This book is dedicated to my students of real estate investing, various mentors and the "success team" I've assembled to help me in business. Without them over the past 39 years I would be thinking at this time about retirement from the saw mill job I secured in Scotia, California when I turned eighteen.

Among those that need special recognition are my mother, Maxine Loyd, and dad, Harold Loyd, who taught me the value of work ethic. Without their example I would never have realized the value of taking commitments so seriously and the importance of completing a job once started. Of course, thanks for the much needed forms of correction, spankings, too.

Claude Powell, Jr., of Colorado taught me the business of residential building. I want to thank him for his friendship and guidance. After 30 years, we are still very close friends and enjoy a mutual admiration society. He is like a brother.

My son, Kevin Loyd, continues to be a balanced source of encouragement and pride. I love working with him and I look forward to our times of brainstorming. He is a thrill for me to have around. I wish every Dad and son could have a relationship like ours.

I can't forget Becky, my wife, who puts up with me. Over the last 38 years together we have been broke and we have been in the money. The latter is better but she has stood by me and supported me (if only publically sometimes). She can give me a good chewing out, but watch out if you try to. Every man needs a good wife like that.

Don Loyd

Table of Contents

All our dreams
can come true - if
we have the courage
to pursue them.

Walt Disney

Introduction

If you want to make a lot of money and benefit from passive income, real estate investing (REI) may be your winning ticket. Like any other business REI is a business that has to be worked. If you think you can read a book and become rich without putting a plan into action, you are wrong. You need a system in place that will help you take advantage of REI or you might keep spinning your wheels and get no where fast.

Some of my protégées have been able to achieve a level of success without knowing why or how success happened. For them success was unpredictable. To take pleasure in continued success, mastery of REI techniques should be condensed to a written system in which the results of your efforts are predictable. Your system will produce consistent and reliable results.

As you read books, listen to speakers, attend workshops, and practice your trade, you will experiment with differing strategies as you apply knowledge gained. The result will be the refinement of your way of doing business. Real estate success is not simply a one-time event—it is an ongoing process. And that process involves refining a formula born from your positive experiences.

Any success you achieve that cannot be replicated is not true success. I designed this book to help you gather information about real estate in general. I offer a system and philosophy for REI. The system is easy to use, and if followed will result in creation of wealth and passive cash flow. You can personalize my system to fit whatever your needs. Feel free to change some of my words if others fit you better. The main concern is for you to enjoy REI success.

Success in real estate does take time and effort. Anyone who suggests otherwise is not telling you the truth. There can be financial risk in REI. But there is risk in doing nothing, too. To minimize REI risk, use proven systems that allow you to create wealth while operating your REI with minimum effort. All it takes is good, solid effort and application of investment principals on your part.

First you need to build a solid foundation upon which to build. Get the information and mindset you need, and then construct the structure of your system as you gain familiarity with real estate. Information comes from expanding your knowledge and wisdom base. Adopt a mindset that mandates success. Whatever you think about it is true. If you think you can do it, then you are correct. If you believe it is impossible, again you are correct.

With those two things in place, your system soon takes over and becomes a part of you, and success takes a life of its own. The secret is to not give up but keep your eye on the prize. In this book, I'll encourage you to do great things as well as give you ideas and suggestions on how to do great things.

We really have a great REI market. If you are ready, you can create wealth. It is up to you. Here's to your success.

Don Loyd

Chapter 1

Cashing In—How to Create Long-Term Income

The opportunities available for real estate investors are unbelievable. Not since the early 1980s have we seen such an array of wealth building, cash flowing properties. Almost everywhere you turn you can find sellers truly motivated to sell. Many homeowners now have "I know I'm going to lose money." mindset. That fact is unfortunate for those in that position but a windfall for those who can make an educated decision and take action.

The current real estate market is a prime opportunity to cash in. Real estate is a better investment today than a year ago and here are four points to consider if you want to safely cash in to create wealth and positive cash flow.

"Cashing In" - Point 1

The 2007 to 2008 real estate market enables you to purchase houses well below value. Foreclosures are occurring at an ever-increasing rate. One way to cash in is to market to

the people who are in foreclosure. This can be done by mailing a series of letters or post cards to those whose homes have had an action from the lender placed on the property. This information is public and readily available.

It may be possible to find a seller who will let you bring the mortgage current and deed you the property. That means you purchase "subject to" the existing financing. The seller's loan stays in place. You can sell it for a quick, small profit, you can hold it long term and do a lease option, or you can simply rent it. You will need to have money to bring the owner current on his mortgage or find a partner who will provide the funds while you put the transaction together and maintain the property.

"Cashing In" - Point 2

Closely associated with point 1, buying homes by way of a "short sale" is a way to generate huge sums of cash. When you purchase a short sale you are, with the approval of the owner, dealing directly with the lender. You make your offer to the owner and deal with what is called the loss mitigation department of the bank.

The downside for you, as the investor, however, in doing a short sale is that it may take several months to get the deal completed. I have had short sales fall through while they were in escrow, and I thought I had a "done deal." Another downside is that you may have to have large sums of money (or a way to get huge sums) to close a short sale. There are several variations and obstacles to short sales. One constant is the paperwork the bank requests when you make an offer. If short sales are your ticket, be sure to read up on how to put them together so the bank will say "yes." At the end of this chapter I recommend resources for you to check out.

As foreclosures increase, lenders will be under greater pressure to off-load the bad loans. It costs a lender about $60,000 to take back a house. In addition, each foreclosure on their books makes it more difficult for them to make loans. Much of their income is derived through closing loans. If their ability to originate loans is decreased, so is their income.

The downside for the owner of the property is he will have to move and lose all equity. He may have additional expenses as well. If the bank forgives $50,000 in debt, that amount may be considered additional income to the seller on which he can be taxed. I understand there is a bill before Congress that will change this tax issue—and rightly so.

The upside is that you purchase a property $.50 to $.60 on the dollar. That could translate into immediate profit and/or positive cash flow. Before you purchase any property use the Don Loyd Rich System™. And be sure to ask:

(1) How much wealth does this property create the day I close escrow?

(2) How much money out of my pocket will it take to close escrow?

(3) When do I get that money back?

(4) Does it have a positive cash flow? If you can answer these questions to your satisfaction you may have a deal.

"Cashing In" - Point 3

In good times or bad, if you understand basic fix-up and repair techniques you will go a long way toward creating wealth. But if you focus your investing attention toward buying and rehabilitating property, you have created a separate business apart from REI. I define investing as a vehicle for your money and/or imagination to do the work of creating wealth and positive cash flow.

The downside to buying and rehabilitating is that you can have a large amount of cash out of pocket in a project. You make a down payment on the house and you also have to use your cash to do the repairs. If you are trying to sell for retail, it might take months to recoup your investment so you can do it all over again.

Another downside is that unless you are an expert in structural design or remodel, you may be getting into a project that will actually cost you more money to fix up than the project is worth. Be very careful. I have been around construction all my life, and I don't do rehabilitation projects any longer because I always made more money as an investor.

The upside is you may have created a job for yourself. Some people like that. They enjoy tearing out sheetrock and remodeling a house. In doing so, it is possible to realize huge returns for your time and investment of cash. I have a list of rehabilitation people who will buy my house at a wholesale price, and they will fix it up and sell for retail. If you want to get into the rehabilitation business let me know, and I will add you to my list.

"Cashing In" - Point 4

You can use all the above to buy and hold. I have changed my REI strategy as a result of our current market. I'm a big proponent of a 1-year lease/option strategy. But in my neck of the woods real estate prices have retreated. I'm now thinking that I want to hold my property for 3 to 5 years instead of 1 so that I can enjoy greater appreciation later.

The downside to such a strategy is that I have become a landlord—something I don't like. I have hired property managers to find tenants and manage the property, but I'm still the one they call if there's a problem. Another downside is I have to wait longer for my equity and being a landlord exposes me to additional liability.

The upside is that as I've been thinking about how to handle the problems of being a landlord I have developed a strategy that will help ease the burden by creating a homeowner mindset in my tenants. I want them to believe that if they pay me on time and take care of the little stuff I will make it possible for them to purchase the house they are living in or another one of my properties if they prefer.

If I successfully accomplish my goal, not only will I have good-paying, quiet tenants, I will have also built-in buyers for future homes. That equates to more cash flow for me and greater opportunities for creating wealth.

Holding the property longer also add another upside. I have more tax deductions. It's possible to take more depreciation, deduct taxes, interest—all the normal tax advantages of rental property. Be sure to talk with your tax advisor and get the latest information.

In conclusion

There are several good resources available to help you learn about cashing in on today's real estate bargains. Peter Conti and David Finkle, authors of *Buying Real Estate Without Cash or Credit* is a book I recommend. They offer sound solutions for buying and selling in this market. Peter Conti also authored *Making Big Money Investing in Foreclosures Without Cash or Credit,* which is worth reading.

I also recommend Wendy Patton's book, *Investing in Real Estate With Lease Options and Subject-To Deals.* Wendy does an excellent job of breaking down the subject into small bite size pieces.

Bill Bronchick offers good insight when he wrote the book, *Flipping Properties—Generate Instant Cash Profits in Real Estate.*

You can also order my book, *Creating Wealth for Women, at* www.CreatingWealthForWomen.net. It outlines a strategy of wealth creation for women and ideas about how to achieve your goals. All you need to do is decide what you want, get some education, set some goals, reduce your goals to a plan, and then work your plan.

We gain strength, and courage, and confidence by each experience in which we really stop to look fear in the face ... we must do that which we think we cannot.

Eleanor Rososevelt

Chapter 2

How to Thrive In a Slowing Market

Many of my REI protégées are new to investing. Until recently, they could purchase anything locally and be assured of a quick profit. They could make bad choices and still look good. Some of those same people are now feeling the pinch of reality as the local market slows to a more normal rate.

Having been in robust markets that have cooled to a recession level (a recession being when <u>they</u> lose money, a depression being when <u>I</u> do), I know there are certain things professional real estate investors can do to prosper in any market. Here are my seven steps:

Have a Plan

The first step is to have a plan. If you don't have a plan, you are planning to fail – as the saying goes. Having a plan assumes you have clearly defined, written out goals. If you work your plan on a daily basis you will create wealth as you achieve your goals. Included in your plan should be time for business, family, and spiritual—don't forget the spiritual part of the equation. It brings the whole into balance.

Make a Schedule

The second step is to work a schedule. If you want to prosper, make a schedule and keep to it. Plan your day. You want to control events rather than have them control you. Have a fixed time each day for such activities as prospecting when you do not take phone calls, rescheduling appointments, and going to real estate closings. You will create more wealth if you discipline yourself to follow that simple second step.

Prioritize Your Activity

The third step is to prioritize. Not all activity on your schedule is of the same level of importance. Do the most important thing first and work down your list. If you have to find the funds to close a transaction, keep at it until finish the task. Tasks with less importance can be delegated to an assistant. My assistant relieves me of so much work it is unbelievable.

Work Only With Motivated Sellers and Qualified Buyers

The fourth step is to only spend time talking to motivated sellers and qualifying your prospects. It is a waste of time to talk to sellers who are really not motivated. In the inflated equity of our local market, many have put their houses up for sale simply to see what will happen hoping to get lucky. If a seller is not motivated, the results can be discouraging and a waste or your time.

Don't waste the buyer's time either. It is fairly easy to determine if a buyer is serious or simply dreaming. It is okay to have them dream on your time as long as you are secure knowing that you can help them achieve the dream.

Education

The fifth step is to take time each day to further your education. Learn different techniques that will make you a better buyer, seller, negotiator, entrepreneur, closer, or that will bring you up to date with various markets and trends. I spend the first hour of each morning increasing my real estate knowledge. At the gym each morning you will find me reading another book on an investment-related subject while doing my cardio workout.

Attitude

The sixth step involves having a right kind of attitude. The fact is, bad things will happen during the day. The question becomes, will it control you, or will you deal with the bad stuff and make something good out of it?

All of us face circumstances we were not planning. What helps make you successful is how you handle the unexpected. I embrace the philosophy that says there is good in all situations—you simply have to look for it. If a deal turns into a lemon I will try to make lemonade with it, sell it, and create wealth.

Plan to Give

The seventh step involves an idea that has been relegated to the rear of the philosophical bus. Most books and articles that tell us how to be successful are focused on "me." They are all about what *I* want, when *I* want it. I think that is dead wrong. If you want to truly enjoy success you must first learn how to give away your wealth to others.

The principle of reciprocity is quite real. The more you give, the more you get. I suggest that you learn to give away at least 10 percent of whatever you earn. If you cannot do that, your wealth owns you rather than you owning it. You can give to a charitable cause (you may even want to start one), educational foundations, or mission projects. The list is endless. Just give it with the thought of not receiving anything in return.

The result will be a satisfying, rich life. I give to others to enrich their lives. I not only share my wealth but also my time. For example, I donate Fridays to helping budding real estate investors. Learn to give and you'll be amazed at the results.

You can survive and even thrive in a slowing market. You just have to work smarter and plan for your success. Follow my seven steps and you will do well.

When I hear somebody sigh

that Life is hard, I am always

tempted to ask,

Compared to what?

Sydney J. Harris

Chapter 3

How to Create Real Estate Wealth Without Owning It.

The current real estate climate is an exciting one. It is because, arguably, more wealth can be created now using less cash than in the past year or two. Many sellers and landlords who wouldn't even listen to a creative way to do a real estate transaction 6 months ago are now eager to hear how creative you can be.

Those who have followed my writing and coaching know that I'm a big proponent of a lease/option method of controlling real estate. "Controlling real estate" is the operative word here. Why not control it rather than own it? "But," you protest, "I thought I had to own real estate to benefit from it." Not so!

The real estate market in is full of empty homes in which the owner is making payments he doesn't want to make. We have a window of opportunity that can result in huge financial gains for the investor who'll work and think outside the box. Consider the following questions:

Q – Why should I buy property by way of a lease/option?

A – You can create wealth and positive cash flow. Owners of empty homes are eager to fill their homes. They are tired of making payments on something that may be, in their eyes losing money and value. You are their savior.

For as little as $100 for option consideration on a 2-year option period (the least amount of time you prefer to negotiate), you can control a house. I have protégées who have secured a 1-year option for the grand total of $1. One person in my real estate investment club will give $1,000 option consideration for a 5-year option.

If you are wondering if that is a good deal for you, consider how much that property may increase in 5 years. As you will read below in a following answer, the $1,000 option consideration (or however much you spend) should be returned to you soon after you have given it.

Q – Why would a seller give you a lease with option to buy?

A – You offer to take care of his property, maintain it properly, pay your payment on time, and have a buyer ready to finance the property at the end of the option period. If you have a 2- to 5-year option (negotiate the longest term possible), he retains all the tax benefits of owning the property and doesn't have to pay a real estate broker fee. In real estate broker fee savings alone he will realize many thousands of dollars.

Q – How and when do you make money?

A – Money is created for the investor at three points in the process. You, the investor, will sublet the house with an option to purchase to a Tenant/Buyer and create cash income. Your 2-year option consideration was $100. You will receive $5,000 on a 1-year option you negotiate with your Tenant/Buyer. You have, therefore, gained $4,900. That amount will be deducted from the sale price if the Tenant/Buyer exercises his option and purchases the home. Here's some great news: You will not have to claim the $4,900 on your income tax until the option of your buyer is exercised or expires.

If you negotiate a rental fee of $1,200 each month from your seller (part of which will be credited to you later) and you find a Tenant/Buyer who will pay you $1,400, you have created positive cash flow of $200. If you control 10 properties in that manner, you'll enjoy a monthly passive income of $2,000. It is also possible to offer your Tenant/Buyer an incentive for giving you additional income. For example, you can offer him a $200 credit for each $100 he pays extra each month. He makes money, and you increase your monthly cash flow.

The third way you can make money is by negotiating an option price of, for example, $250,000, and selling to your Tenant/Buyer for $270.000. If you do this, you will have created $20,000 plus at least $2,400 per house for the year. And you did it without owning the property or qualifying for a loan.

Q – How do you find motivated sellers?

A – Marketing is the key to any business. There is no exception. You must have contacts to stay in business. You can make a lot of money if you will spend a minimum of 1 hour each day working your marketing plan.

Lease/option sellers can be found by going to the library and looking back 2 or 3 months in the real estate classifieds for houses for rent. If a property owner has been making payments on an empty house for that long, you may have a motivated seller.

Call the number of the owner (I normally skip the property management companies, but they might be open to a call as well) and ask if the house is still available for rent. If it is, have him tell you about it. Then, tell him that you are interested in a long-term lease of at least 2 years. Ask if that is something that may be of interest to him.

If he is not interested in leasing for 1 year, thank him for his time and wish him well. If he is interested, tell him you are an investor and ask if you pay your rent on time and take care of his property, would he be willing to sell it to you when the lease is up.

If he answers in the affirmative, you may have a lease option. You then meet him and look at the house. If the house will serve your purpose, negotiate a lease-option arrangement that benefits you.

Here are some other ways to find motivated seller: If you see an empty house, note the address and contact your title company or county clerk for ownership information. Write a letter to the owner offering to lease option his house. Do some research in writing sales letters and make a extremely compelling argument. Be sure to explain how he will benefit. He must clearly understand what's in it for him.

If you have a real estate broker team member (your success team), have the team member send you the daily list of expired listings. Write each one a letter using the formula in the above paragraph. Be sure your broker is compensated in some manner. Most real estate brokers will jump through hoops for you if they know they will get paid at some point.

Real estate brokers are also a great source for finding motivated sellers. Educate your broker or brokers on the subject of lease options and how they could benefit. A payday several months away is much better than no payday at all.

Q – What kind of documents should I use?

A– If you are buying on a lease option, you need a simple one-page lease option form. Keep it simple and to the point. You can buy on online, at my office, or have your attorney draw one up for you. Just make sure the document is buyer friendly.

When you're selling, use a much more comprehensive lease and option agreement. The one I use (you can purchase and download it at www.RealCashFlow.net and go to "Products") has many protections for the seller. Those two documents (the lease and option) have taken away all my landlord headaches. I don't have any calls for repairs or complaints.

Q – How do I safeguard myself?

If you're going to buy with a lease option here is a list of things you may need:

1. A signed Authorization to Release Information form for the lender. You want to know that your seller is making his payments each month. You don't want to discover the house is in foreclosure.

2. You may want to set up an escrow account. The escrow company will collect the payment and disburse the funds. If you set up an escrow account, be sure to have the seller sign a Warranty Deed and place it in escrow to be released when you are ready to exercise your option and purchase the property. If the seller is vacationing in China when you get ready to close your loan, you won't have to go look for him.

3. Your option agreement should include provisions describing what happens if your seller fails to make a payment or pay the property taxes. The document I use states that I have the option of making his payment. If I do make the payment, my option agreement states I will be credited $3 (it could just as easily be $4 for every dollar) I spend on his behalf.

In other words, if he doesn't make his $1,500 per month payment and I do, $4,500 will be credited to me when I exercise my option to purchase. Not a bad return on my $1,500 and he is motivated to keep his payment current. If my landlord is late on 10 payments, I may be able to deduct up to $45,000 off the price of the house.

There is money to be made using lease options. If you haven't already explored that option for controlling property, you should. Think outside the box and let the deals happen. You will be pleasantly surprised at what you can do.

The individual who know the score about life sees difficulties as opportunities.

Norman Vincent Peale

Chapter 4

How to Find Motivated Sellers

Professional real estate investors don't waste time with properties selling for retail. There is no money in that. They look for distressed properties in which a buyer must be located as soon as possible. The most common reasons owners need to sell are death, divorce, job loss, job transfer, an increased interest rate on an adjustable mortgage, or because the seller is supporting two or more properties.

Here are eight ways to find motivated sellers. You can use all of them or choose one that fits your personal style so you achieve your personal investment goals and objectives.

1. Follow Foreclosure Notices

In most local newspapers, you will find a section containing legal notices. Before a lender can foreclose on a traditional loan, however, they have to give public notice of the default. Your county clerk will have foreclosure information available. Armed with that information, you can contact the owner and try to negotiate a purchase.

Many title companies offer a free monthly service that provides information about foreclosures. Some companies are better than others in assisting the investor. I use my local branch of First American Title Company. They work hard to provide not only default notices filed but also supporting documentation. They also do their best to provide me with anything else that may help. Explore the service options available to you at your local title company. You will be pleasantly surprised.

Two friends and I have a stand-alone company (TLC Real Estate Solutions, LLC) that actually "markets" the foreclosure marketplace. For a small monthly fee, we subscribe to a service that not only lists foreclosures but also provides services such as comparables, pre-written letters and post cards, and a marketing strategy. The company is My Realty Data. You can preview the service by going to www.oaprei.com/Products/ and clicking on the left link that says, "Real Estate Investing on Steroids." I have high praise for the service.

2. Out-of-Area Owners

People who live outside the area are a great target as well as a great niche. You can find them easily by requesting a list of out-of-area owners from your local county clerk (you may have to do the legwork and research) or by contacting the customer service representative at your favorite title company.

The title company I use provides that information in minutes. I can have it faxed, e-mailed, or delivered to my office. They will even print mailing labels for the owners if I request that they do so. Once equipped with the information (and tools), I begin a direct-mail campaign to the out-of-area owners. In that mailing, I include an update of our local real estate market and an offer to buy their property. I make it easy for them to respond—and they do respond. There have been times when the owners had an empty house, and they didn't have a clue what they were going to do with it. I show them how I can help remove their headaches and hassles by giving them to me.

3. Expired Listings

I believe each real estate investor should have a real estate broker on his or her team. One reason is simple—you gain access to the information on the local Multiple Listing Service (MLS). Ask your broker for a list of expired listings. I have updated information available each day. I know on Tuesday that a listing ended on Monday, and I can contact the owners and offer them a solution to their problem.

Some real estate brokers review MLS expired listing inventory all the time in an attempt to re-list one or more expired listing. Why shouldn't you contact them? When a property has been on the market for an extended period of time, it's usually because the property is overpriced. Depending on motivation, the owner may be willing to get realistic with the price and lower it simply to get rid of it. That has happened before, so be sure you try the approach.

4. Place a Classified Ad

Give notice to the community that you want to buy any house in any condition at any price. I personally don't do this (it's not my niche), but I know many who do. The reports I get back are a mixed bag. If an investor has a plan, and one aspect of his marketing plan is a classified ad, the ad works.

The successful investors I know who place classified ads are not bombarded with phone calls, but they do a few transactions a year and that justifies the cost. Those who place a classified ad on a whim—without a plan—don't appear to do well. My guess is they are shooting in the dark, hoping if they spend enough money something will stick. You have to have a plan, incorporate that plan into your daily activity, and then manage the activity.

5. Bandit Signs

You see the signs all the time: "I Buy Houses, Any Price, Any Condition," or words to that effect followed by a phone number. Bandit signs do work. The goal with any marketing plan for finding motivated sellers is getting the seller to call you. Bandit signs can accomplish that goal.

Bandit signs are inexpensive to purchase and easy to distribute. One downside is a growing number of local governments threatening to fine anyone who posts such signs. If you decide to use bandit signs, check your local regulations. Make sure you are not opening yourself up to a costly fine.

6. For Sale by Owner

In the classified section of your local paper, you will find ads placed by motivated sellers. They sometimes say, "For Sale by Owner." Often referred to as FISBOs, you may also find the ads on Internet sites that market to FISBOs. I used to read the classified section every day looking for FISBO ads. If they use the words, "Must Sell," "Owner Motivated," "Owner Terms," or similar expressions, they are a good candidate to contact.

Usually the FISBO is a less sophisticated seller. They are trying on their own to either save the real estate commission (which rarely happens), or they don't have enough equity to pay a sales fee. In either case, when they boldly proclaim: "For Sale by Owner," they are begging you to call them. Don't let them down. I have made some of my best deals responding to a FISBO ad.

7. Hire a Bird Dog

A "Bird Dog" is a person you offer a finder's fee to if they bring you a seller (or buyer). Let this person know what you are looking for and turn him loose. For example, let your friends know what you are doing and tell them you will pay a fee (decide on a fair amount). How about your neighbors or family? Everyone you come in contact with is a potential "Bird Dog." Use your imagination and talk to people regularly.

8. "Farm" an Area

Farming is a term real estate brokers use when they flood a specific geographical area or mailing route in the hope of becoming the "recognized real estate expert" in that area. Used as part of a long-term strategy, farming works well.

If you want to "farm," do monthly post card mailings. Let the neighborhood know who you are and how you can help. The cost can literally be pennies per household each month. The return on that investment has great potential.

For information on direct mail marketing of real estate, you might want to check out Richard Roop, who specializes in it and has written some excellent articles you can download free of charge. His Web site is www.RichardRoop.com.

Now Just Do It!

Now that you have some basic information, decide what you will do. Build a detailed plan that addresses your area of interest. Break down that plan into daily activity. Then, work the plan. See the big picture, know what is there, and focus on the daily activity by managing your time in an effective way. If you follow those steps, you are sure to succeed.

Stand up to your obstacles and do something about them. You will find that they haven't half the strength you think they have.

Norman Vincent Peale

Chapter 5

No More Sleepless Nights

There were times back in the early 80s I had difficulty going to sleep at night. Business was terrible during those bleak years and almost everyone was experiencing a tough financial situation. I was doing my best to sell and build houses and the market was ... well ... not exactly in the tank—the "tank" had flat disappeared.

During this time my wife let me know that she was upset about the fact that we had lost "everything" as she put it. I pointed out to her that we had not lost everything. We had:

1. good health,
2. two healthy kids who happened to be great kids,
3. new education and experiences,
4. a wonderful support system, and
5. friends and family who truly loved us—just to name a few positive things.

In fact, the only thing we lost was a few houses (that we had no real money into), some cash (which was replaceable), and a newer Cadillac (then with about 70,000 miles which we traded for a Chrysler Cordoba with 40,000 miles).

When I stepped back to take a look, I didn't see the rubble of a crumbling personal financial statement. I saw the good things and the things that really mattered.

We started in 1969 with nothing in the bank and no property. Our assets consisted of a wedding ring. Since I was making payments on a student loan and car, we started off financially upside down. We had come a long way in a short time.

Thirteen years later we still had no money in the bank—it was all gone. But we did have the house we were living in, which carried a truly great interest rate of 12 percent on an owner carry loan—not 14 or 15 percent like every other contemporary home buyer.

Of course, we had the good health, great kids, new education, and wonderful support system of which I wrote earlier. In addition to all the good things we walked away with, we had also enjoyed a great ride. And man, the ride was terrific.

Over time I have learned not to allow business events out of my control to rob me of sleep. Having a good life is more important than having a successful subdivision or a portfolio full of rental property. We truly do have a lot to be thankful in spite of the current rotten real estate market if we will be silent long enough to listen and do a little positive counting.

Counting sheep might not help you fall asleep but counting your blessings may be your ticket. It was mine.

My advice to you is simple: do the best you can today and not worry over the events and markets you cannot correct. I try to do the best I can on any given day, and I don't worry about things I am powerless to direct.

I now figure if events and the market are out of my control, whether I sleep or not is a moot point. I fall asleep today as easily as a baby. All the lost sleep will not change one thing except assist in declining health.

Chapter 6

Time to Benefit from Sub-Prime Loans

Mortgage lending has tightened in recent weeks. Many of us who were qualified for a real estate investment loan discovered that, much to our dismay, we no longer qualified for the loan that made sense for us to invest in certain kinds of real estate transactions.

In fact, to be more precise, the loan we wanted was no longer available. Period! Thankfully, the real estate lending picture is looking much brighter. Programs that were not available 1 or 2 weeks ago are again available—and more are coming on line at an encouraging pace. The reason for the quick turnaround in lending philosophy is simple. The lenders discovered their knee jerk reaction to foreclosures in the sub-prime market did not correctly reflect the paying habits of Alt A type borrowers (most of us who have great credit and plenty of income but choose to apply for a loan using stated income).

The sub-prime loan market is a different breed of loan and target audience. The rates and fees are higher for sub-

prime loans because the applicants are a greater risk. They either do not make enough money to qualify in the normal way or they do not pay their bills in a timely fashion, or both. Lenders make an educated guess about the reliability of these borrowers. Sometimes they the get it right, sometimes they do not. But the point is, sub-prime borrowers are not a great risk.

The positive side to the mortgage "meltdown," as I recently saw it called, is that it has created a wonderful climate for REI. Now is the time to educate yourself and jump in. In the next 60 to 90 days, millions of dollars will be made for real estate investors.

The herd mentality will result in freighted homeowners willing to pay for you to take their property on your terms. Is there risk in investing? Yes. But if you can buy or control property without using your hard-earned cash, you have very little risk.

Jameson Frank wrote: "the greatest battles are that with our own minds." The choice is yours. You can be a sheep and follow the herd or you can take the bull by the horns and reap tremendous profits virtually risk free. The only question is will you be ready to reap the rewards of bad press coverage and scare tactics? Now, go make it a great REI day. It's your choice.

Chapter 7

How to Earn an Amazing Income

You need monthly cash flow if your goal is to quit your day job and enjoy a life of independence from the daily "9 to 5" grind. I will show you how controlling property through a Lease Option will bring in the monthly cash needed to quit the "day job" and building new homes will give you regular large sums ($30,000 to $50,000 or more) of cash you can invest or put away. In accomplishing those two goals, you'll also be able to work at home if you wish.

There's something gratifying about knowing you don't have to rush around in the morning to get to work. For many years, I worked from home and enjoyed the independent lifestyle. Imagine how it must feel! You get up in the mornings and you only have to walk down the hall to your office. You open the door, sit down at your desk, and your day begins. How would it feel to you if you had no commute? How much extra time would you have for family activities?

Having trained hundreds of real estate investors on the subject of Lease Options (or Lease Purchase—same thing), I know that operating a Lease Purchase home-based business can be very rewarding and very inexpensive to set up. You will need a phone, fax, computer, and Internet access. All of those tools are very easy to secure. You probably have the items already. You will rarely have to leave your home office if you operate your business correctly.

You can do your personal seller prospecting using the phone, fax, and e-mail. After you secure a house to sell by way of Lease Purchase, you will take the all the calls from your prospective Buyer/Tenant when they respond to your classified ads.

How do I get monthly income?
First, you find a motivated seller. In this case, it's most likely an existing, frustrated landlord. He's been making payments on an empty house, or he doesn't have the mental preparedness to deal with tenants. For him, the vacant house is a cash drain and he simply wants to get rid of his problem. You make a deal for the house using a Lease Purchase agreement. You negotiate a sales price at the end of the option period, a monthly lease payment and the right to sub-lease (also called a sandwich lease).

The Sales Price
If the seller demands current value for the house, you negotiate a 5-year, or more, option period. Even in slow markets 5 years should be long enough for the house to increase in value. In hot markets you can make even more money.

If you can negotiate a discounted sales price, a minimum of 2 years for an option period should be acceptable for you. You want a discount because you want to be able to add money for you. If the your option purchase price is $300,000, you want your buyer to agree to an option purchase price of $325,000 or $350,000. You have to earn equity.

The Monthly Payment

If the market is slow, and the seller has a huge monthly payment, the seller may have to bite the bullet and pay part of his payment. Remember you have to have positive cash flow in order to survive. You want to realize at least $100 to $200 each month in income. If his payment is $1,800 a month, and you can lease it for $1,200, you want your monthly lease payment to be $1,000. The seller has to make up the additional $800.

Why would a seller agree to this arrangement? Because he has a ton on equity in the house, and he wants retail for his house, but it is bleeding him dry. He's desperate and he needs you to help him. But be prepared to walk away from a deal. He needs you more than you need him.

The Option Consideration

Option consideration is a nonrefundable sum of money that gives the buyer the right, but not the obligation, to purchase the house.

You're the Buyer

Your purchase amount is predetermined (or a formula that arrives at a price) at the end of the option period. If you are buying by way of a Lease Purchase, you want the option money to be as little as possible. Some of my protégés have secure 1-year options for as little as $1. Others have secured 5-year options for $1,000. When buying through a Lease Purchase agreement, agree to as little option money as possible. Each dollar you spend here means you could make less nonrefundable cash when you sell.

You're the "Seller"

You want to get as much as possible from your Tenant/Buyer in option consideration. This is cash flow you can spend. You can pay bills, take a vacation, or invest it in other property. It allows you to get back the money you spent on the original option price. I teach my protégés to ask for a minimum of $5,000. Most of the time they get that much or more. One recently received $20,000 in option consideration. I had a family who waffled back and forth, "Our problem is," they said to me, "should we give you $100,000 or $200,000." I was asking for $5,000 "or best offer." They wanted to give the "best offer."

Here's a little extra added benefit: option consideration is not a taxable event (in other words, you don't pay taxes) until the option is exercised or expires. That means you can use the full amount without being taxed for a year or more.

As you can see, there's a tremendous opportunity in the Lease Purchase market. Pursuing prospective sellers is as simple as contacting owners who have rental properties listed in your local newspaper classified ads. Go to your local library and look at classified ads from 2 or 3 months ago. Call the landlord and ask if the house is still available. If it is, you have a motivated landlord. Then tell him your interested in a lease of at least 2 years and if that's something that may be acceptable (what do you think he's doing? Although you can't see him, he's responding like Pavlov's dog). You can then tell him you are a real estate investor and would like to buy the home at the end of the lease—would that be something he'd be open to? If he says yes, you have a Lease Purchase prospect.

Eileen Bronchick, the Chief Operations Officer of LegalWiz Publications said, *Don Loyd is the real deal when it comes to real estate investing. Follow his time tested principles and you will succeed in creating wealth.* **Creating Wealth for Women** *is an essential resource for achieving your investing goals.*

If I were asked to give what I consider the single most useful bit of advice for all humanity, it would be this: Expect trouble as an inevitable part of life, and when it comes, hold your head high. Look it squarely in the eye, and say, "I will be bigger than you. You cannot defeat me.

Ann Landers

Chapter 8

Where's Your Best Investment?

Where should you put your investment dollars today? Is real estate a good vehicle or is something else better? Investing falls into two basic investment types. You can invest in paper or you can invest in real estate. Paper investments include just about everything except real estate. Even bullion, rare coins, and art work could be considered paper investments. I include them in this category because, unlike real estate that has regular cash flow, they are assets that have no regular cash flow. You have to sell them in order to realize any return on cash investment.

The major difference between investing in real estate or any paper investment boils down to a fundamental principle: leverage. Let's say that you have $50,000 to invest. You can read books, take a course, search the internet, talk to brokers and do all the due diligence required to invest in a stock.

You find a stock you like and purchase it. You take $50,000 and purchase the appropriate number of shares. If the stock increases 10 percent in value over the course of a year, you have a return of $5,000. Not a bad investment. You enjoy a 10-percent return on your cash investment.

Here's the big difference in real estate in very simple terms. You take that same $50,000 and you can purchase a property with a value of $250,000. You purchase the property and put 20 percent down ($50,000). You secure a loan for $200,000 and find a tenant who will make your payment. Assuming the same 10-percent appreciation in asset you would enjoy a return of $25,000. In other words your return on cash investment would be 50 percent rather than 10 percent.

This is what's referred to as leverage. Interestingly, you can actually do much better than 10 percent if you shop wisely. If you find a motivated seller, you could possibly enjoy more than a 100-percent return on your cash investment. You can find a motivated seller who will now sell a $250,000 house for $200,000. My company regularly makes offers of $.50 on the dollar—using very little cash in the process. How's that for leverage?

Which 10-percent return would rather have? Remember you can outsource property management and maintenance. I do. If you build a good "Success Team," it can help you find good buys on property and loans with favorable terms. If you build your team right, you can also learn ways to buy real estate using little of your own cash making your investments virtually risk free. On top of all that, you can qualify for some very favorable tax incentives for investing in real estate, which will lower your tax burden and you enjoy more spendable cash.

Author Bill Bronchick, Nationally recognized Real Estate Attorney and investor writes:

If you want to make a ton of money in real estate investing, you need to read Don Loyd's new book, Creating Wealth for Women. He shows you how he did it and how you can do it, too. His step by step approach is a safe and sound. His four question plan in analyzing investment property can result in huge financial gains. Don has proven he has the ability and experience to create wealth with little or no cash out of pocket. Now he shares his success story with the general public and invites you along for a great ride.

Difficulties should act as a tonic.
They should spur us to greater
exertion.

B. C. Forbes

Chapter 9

The Secret to Real Estate Success in an Adjusting Market

One thing that makes real estate so interesting and profitable is the cyclical nature of it. There are times of boom where everything in sight explodes as costs rise into the stratosphere as everyone, it seems, just jumps in hoping to cash in on the good times while they roll. Then there are times of price stagnation in which price reductions may occur as the markets adjusts to the lack of demand. And then, once every few decades, property is almost worthless in some areas.

We have heard a lot about a coming real estate crash. The doomsayers are predicting a total collapse of real estate prices. Are they right? Anything is possible, but probably not! Too much depends on real estate.

Our ever-increasing population will have to live somewhere, and the power brokers in Washington, D.C., have vested interests in helping maintain some semblance of balance. REI can be risky business. But if history is a good measure, prices will go up and down— but mostly they will go up.

Professional real estate investors do well regardless of what any given market does. They make adjustments when they identify the tell-tale signs of market changes, which allow them to thrive even in a bad market. Here are four REI secrets investors use that will help you stay ahead of the game.

The Hot Markets

Red Hot Markets don't last forever. There comes a time when all "good things" come to an end. Hot real estate markets are no exception. The true professional will purchase property with an exit strategy that takes into account for the adjusting market by buying in the best locations that will enable them to more easily unload the property when the slow down arrives.

Most professionals see the signs of a crumbling market and start looking for up-and-coming markets and begin the process of getting out of the hot market. That strategy, while no guarantee, will make it possible for an investor to buy in the best areas so they can get out quickly if needed. No one has a crystal ball; they look at things like employment, employment opportunities, real estate demand, rental housing availably and demand, local government, commercial projects, and many other indicators.

As investment opportunities come available, they start buying property in other locations that promise appreciation or profit. Many investors will purchase in several areas so that they can spread their exposure and gain "safe" returns on investments. One area might be slow, or slowing, while another may be experiencing 35-percent, or more, annual appreciation.

The professional will try to get into an area before the location reaches its peak and then sell before the market goes down. That enables them to start buying in an area where they can profit from the next upward trend. Then they may wait for

the former hot market to experience a rush of foreclosures, and they buy properties at a discount and wait for the market to rebound.

The Balance of Supply and Demand

Here's a fundamental fact I want you to remember: When the supply is high, prices go down. When the demand is high, prices go up. There were people in my investment club who believed prices would maintain its rocket speed. The reality is, if there is too much of any type of real estate, prices decline. Even for me! I purchased building lots for $135,000 that I would have a hard time selling for $99,000 today. Obviously, I missed the market and will pay the price.

There comes a point in every market cycle when investors and new buyers dry up. As the demand falls, excess supply cascades to a more natural price level. A direct correlation exists between rental prices and prices for homes. If too much disparity, home prices shrink because investors won't buy a property they have to feed (add additional income to each month) or have a terrible return on their cash investment.

Study the market and determine when the supply outstrips the demand. Then, when you see new buyers light up the home buying market, you will know when to start buying in that area again.

Put the Breaks on Speculation

Speculation is hoping for a profit—just like when you go to a casino and hope to come out with their money. Can you do it? Sometimes, maybe. But the odds are in the favor of the house.

I teach my protégées to make their money when they buy. In other words, they know how much money they've made on the day the loan closes. Know how much money you made on your transaction the day you close, too. Buy it right, realize

your profit when you sell, and you might even get a nice bonus of appreciation or a zone change that increases the value.

Don Loyd's RICH System™ uses a very simple way of evaluating an investment property. If you can't answer the questions below and get good, positive answers, you may not want to invest in a project. Ask yourself:

R – *Return?* – How much wealth does this property create for me today? This is not appreciation or how much you can sell it for next year.
I – *Investment?* – How much money out of my pocket will this take? Normally, I want to put in as little money as necessary.
C – *Cash Back?* – If I put money in, when do I get it back?
The goal is to get your money back as soon as possible so you can do more investing.
H – *Holding Income?* – Does the property have positive cash flow? You want to avoid negative cash flow. It can put you out of business.

This simple formula can be used when considering any investment made by most investors. It's very telling in that it gets to the heart of the issue. Cash and cash flow are vital to the livelihood of investors.

Equity Preservation

Don't easily give up your equity. Protect it to the best of your ability. If you think you have to borrow from your equity pool, borrow from some of your investment properties. I have lines of credit on almost all my homes. I've never tapped into my investment portfolio, but it's there if I need it.

Use great care to protect your personal home. Don't borrow against the equity. It's too valuable a resource to tap into for anything other than short term money. I you are disciplined enough to resist the urge to use your equity for a vacation, new car and such things, I recommend you get a home equity line of credit (also called a HELOC) for short term loans. Your equity for any other use than short term loans exposes your family to unnecessary risk.

History suggests you'll do fine in real estate if you have an investing plan that includes allowances for the up and downs of markets and sound exit strategies. You can do well in bad markets, too. In fact, you can get rich if you know what you are doing. Spend the money it takes to get good education, information, and coaching. It will be money well spent.

Finally, learn to think outside the box of conventional wisdom. Being creative will go a long way toward your success as a real estate investor.

What this power is I cannot say;

all I know is that it exists

and it becomes available

only when a man[or woman]

is in that state of mind

in which he knows exactly

what he wants and is fully

determined not to quit

until he finds it."

Alexander Graham Bell

Chapter 10

Real Estate Investing or Business Plan

Real estate investing, or REI, has been defined in a variety of ways. For some, REI is anything that has to do with purchasing real estate regardless of the nature of the "investment." While you might argue that real estate development is investing, it's also a business separate and apart from investing.

REI in its simplest form is the passive activity of using cash reserves, leverage, or imagination and producing income. In its truest since, REI is not purchasing a property and completing a remodel on a house. Remodeling houses is a business that requires specialized skills, specific knowledge, and a business plan.

I'm a general contractor, among other things. I build houses. If I purchase a building lot and construct a house to sell, I will have invested in a building business, which is not the same as me investing in real estate. Although real estate is

connected to my business activity, I'm not an investor in real estate in that case.

On occasion, I'm involved in the development of building lots for new construction. As a developer I adhere to a business plan to (hopefully) make a profit. The results are, to a large extent, directly related to my business plan and follow through and are market driven. If I make some bad business decisions or if I'm trying to develop building lots in a down market, I may not make any money for that effort and expenses. Or, I may lose money. By the same token, if I make good business decisions and/or I have a sizzling market, I may make millions of dollars.

I have lost money on real estate business activity. In 2006, for example, I purchased a plot of ground I wanted to subdivide and build houses on the building lots. I did the prudent thing and "pre-sold" the entire project before I closed escrow. Each buyer put up $5,000 each for the privilege of securing the right to purchase one of my homes.

With a "sold out" project, I secured a bank loan to build the infrastructure (such as streets, sidewalks, and curbs). Then events beyond my control began to unfold. I found the city impossible to deal with as they added conditions to their original "approval" and long periods of delay, which sent my cost soaring out of control. At one point I was paying about $1,500 per day in interest on vacant ground without final plat approval at a time when the total build out of the homes should have been completed.

To add insult to injury, my buyers began to ask for their deposits back. I promised a construction start date and could not meet it. Mortgage programs disappeared as the worst real estate market in 25 years reared its ugly head. The loans for which my buyers qualified were no longer available. In total, I

stand to lose at least $1,000,000 cash in the project. When the dust settles, the total could reach $2,000,000.

Was my failure one of investing in real estate? The answer is, "absolutely not." I wasn't in a real estate investment; I was involved in the real estate <u>development business.</u>

There are various risks associated with any investment. I think the safest investment is still real estate. When investing in real estate it is possible to enjoy virtually risk-free investments if you use the Don Loyd RICH System™. My RICH System™, as you saw in the previous chapter, involves asking four simple questions and getting back four simple, honest answers. Here they are again:

R – *Return?* – How much wealth does this property create for me today? This is not appreciation or how much you can sell it for next year.
I – *Investment?* – How much money out of my pocket will this take? Normally, I want to put in as little money as necessary.
C – *Cash Back?* – If I put money in, when do I get it back?
The goal is to get your money back as soon as possible so you can do more investing.
H – *Holding Income?* – Does the property have positive cash flow? You want to avoid negative cash flow. It can put you out of business.

Get good, honest answers to these questions ` and you will likely make better choices with fewer loses. As an investor you want to maximize profits and limit losses. To accomplish those two goals, it is incumbent on you to do your best due diligence. Remember that no one is watching out for you with the same interest that you have about your financial health.

Are you in a real estate related business or are you a real life real estate investor? The choice is truly only yours to decide.

Every worthwhile

accomplishment, big or little,

has its stages of drudgery

and triumph;

a beginning,

a struggle

and a victory.

Ghandi

Chapter 11

Finding Profit in OPM (Other People's Money)

When I began investing in real estate, I had no knowledge of how to use OPM (Other People's Money). I didn't know such a thing existed. Today you can find books and articles on the subject in abundance.

As the traditional real estate market of 2007 and 2008 implodes, nontraditional investors will be the ones who help with the clean-up effort by purchasing homes the banks have taken back. In the process, they will be making a lot of money—to a large extent using OPM.

What can you do with OPM?

The basic theory regarding OPM is a simple one. You can earn a very good living (some of the wealthiest people on the planet use OPM to build their fortunes) without using much of your own cash. That means the wealth you create is the result of maximum return on your money. The benefit to you is huge. Because you need little start-up capital and little, or no, credit, you can:

1. achieve amazing cash flow almost immediately
2. have your real estate investment business
3. operational and full time in a short time
4. realize an outstanding and realistic first year income
5. work out of your home and use the "virtual office" arrangement (Google "virtual office").

Using OPM means you view debt as a tool, and some even embrace the idea that OPM may be their best friend. A tool will be good, or bad, depending upon the skill with which the craftsman works the tool. The basic goal of most consumers is to be free of debt. But real estate investors know that there is good debt and bad. Good debt, debt that generates income, is a tool investors can sharpen and learn to use expertly. The reality of using debt responsibly (as in good debt) can earn them huge returns.

Closing associated with OPM is the concept of leverage. Leverage is using a small initial investment with the goal of gaining a high return in relation to the investment. It allows you to control more of investment property while reducing your personal loss. If you purchase a property for $200,000 and you put down $40,000, you have leveraged your investment of $40,000.

Having leverage means you don't have to write a check for the entire $200,000 to realize the return on that amount. If you take your $40,000, invest it in stocks and enjoy a 10 percent rate of return, you will have earned $4,000. If your real estate valued at $200,000 has a 10-percent return, you'll enjoy a return of $20,000. You will have leveraged your money and earned a greater income.

For the latter, you are using OPM. You have borrowed 80 percent of your investment from a bank and leveraged your $40,000. That is an example of what Robert Kiyosaki of *Rich Dad, Poor Dad* fame calls "good debt" because you are creating profit and cash flow. An example of this concept can be seen in Donald Trump, who carries incredible debt as it leverages into more wealth. He is so successful using OPM that people pay staggering sums just to hear him speak.

How OPM can help you?
Beginning and budding real estate investors can take advantage of OPM by using several approaches to investing.

Find a Partner
Let's say you want to invest but don't have any money or credit. The easiest way to tap into this great market is to find a property to purchase at a wholesale price. Prepare a flip chart presentation showing potential investors how they can make significant return on that investment if will partner with you for a real estate flip, rental, or retail sale. Show the investors what is in it for them. Use their money (if needed) and credit (if needed) and you're using OPM and in business tomorrow.

Buy Short Sales

Read up on short sales and find several to make offers on. Learn to negotiate with the lenders and start buying homes. The interesting thing with this approach is you don't have to have partners to for this. You can purchase at wholesale, add a few thousand dollars for yourself, and also sell wholesale to another buyer—leaving plenty of money on the table for your buyer.

Pre-Foreclosure

The pre-foreclosure market is huge. You can bring sellers current on their loans, have the seller deed you the property, and take over the payments (OPM). There are several ways to accomplish that, and I have addressed the approaches in other chapters. But, the major point here is that the bank loan is still in place and you didn't have to qualify for it. Be sure you understand what you're doing. Read everything you can on the subject so you can make an informed decision.

Lease Option

One of my favorite investment strategies is buying and selling via a lease option (also called rent-to-own and Lease Purchase). Using a lease option document to control property is using OPM. For a small fee you are granted an option to buy. You sell for a larger option fee and create cash flow. You also sell higher than your optioned the property, generating future profit. And, you can lease the property for more than your lease amount, provided you negotiated a lower amount when you optioned the property.

Credit Cards

I'm reluctant to include this form of using OPM because of the tremendous danger of new investors finding themselves in a very bad position when things don't work out as they think it should.

Having said that, it's possible to obtain interest-free loans from your credit card if you are careful to repay the loan in a speedy fashion. If you are not disciplined enough, or if the transaction is risky, don't use your credit cards to leverage yourself into a property. I have seen too many people have to go back to work at a job they hate because of a poor choice for using credit and credit cards.

A More Sophisticated Investor

If multimillion dollar projects are your goal, you can use OPM by raising equity. You are back to finding partners, but this time you are looking for "accredited investors." Accredited investors are men and women who have substantial income levels. Briefly, the minimum income is $200,000 a year or assets of at lease $1,000,000.

In this scenario you are trying to raise 30-percent equity, for example, so you can borrow the 70 percent it takes to complete the multimillion dollar commercial or industrial building. You do the due diligence, hire the designers, lawyers, builders, and you answer to your partners who have put up the cash.

If you decide to jump into this arena, you need to take a good class or workshop on the subject. Make sure you understand the law and what you are doing. There are some very strict rules to which you must adhere. Failure to do so might result in you going to jail. The Securities and Exchange Commission takes a dim view of people who ignore their rules. There are even rules about who you can talk with about your project and when you can do it. The upside is that you can earn literally millions of dollars in fees for putting together deals using OPM.

Regardless of your interest in OPM, you can use the process as a tool that can help you break free from the daily grind of a job and just getting by. As with any investment there is risk. I think the most risky thing is to do nothing and wait for someone else to take care of you. But, again, the choice is entirely yours.

Chapter 12

Declining Markets are Great Markets

New investors sometimes complain about declining markets. They believe the news reports that the sky is falling and they will go broke. They may go broke if they have followed the herd and purchased property at elevated retail price levels. But the fact is, soft and declining markets are the best markets in which to invest.

Wendy Patton, a long time real estate investor and a personal favorite of mine, argues the same. In an article entitled, "Why Soft Markets are GREAT Markets," she explains her reasoning.

This is what Wendy, a real professional real estate investor, writes about a soft real estate market:

Investing in real estate has changed in many markets in our country. If you are like me, you live in a real estate market that has gone soft. There are still some areas in the country where homes are appreciating nicely, but nothing like it was in 2000- 2005. There were a lot of self-proclaimed real estate gurus that popped up during the boom times telling you how to make HUGE PROFITS in real estate. Back then, during the up cycle, investing in real estate was so easy. You could throw money at almost any piece of real estate and be practically guaranteed to make a profit. It seemed like anyone who had flipped a couple of houses and made a profit was an "expert" investor.

Times are different now. Investing in real estate takes a little more effort. Investors that haven't weathered down cycles before are struggling because all they know are massively appreciating markets. All too many of those self-proclaimed gurus lost their shirts when the markets changed. Those ads that go "I made $256 million in real estate in 4 weeks with no money down" are a whole lot less believable. Okay, $256 million is an exaggeration, but you know what I mean.

So the questions are now, "How do we still go about investing in real estate and make profits?" Can it be done in these soft markets?"

The answer to those questions is quite simple. I can say that without question, without hesitation, the answer is: YES! ABSOLUTELY!

I have been investing in real estate for more than 20 years. I have seen up cycles and I have seen down cycles. I have made money and been successful in both. I can tell you several things about down markets that may surprise you. First, experienced real estate investors will tell you that more money is made in down markets than in up markets.

It's true, MORE MONEY is made in DOWN markets than in up markets! Second, experienced investors PREFER to do the bulk of their investing in DOWN markets. There are a number of reasons for this but the big ones are there are more motivated sellers in down markets and the competition (other investors) pursuing these motivated sellers is LOWER. It's a double bonus.

Down markets produce more deals and less competition to get those deals.

One of the investing techniques I specialize in is Lease Options. Lease Options are one of the absolute best techniques for investing in real estate in down markets. I'll say it again, if you are looking for ways to get involved with real estate investing you need to know this, Lease Options are one of the absolute best techniques for investing in real estate in down markets. Let's take a look at why.

I've already said down markets produce high numbers of motivated sellers. Right now in Michigan, it's very common to see a house listed on the market in two ways, both for sale and for rent. They are listed this way because the sellers KNOW how bad it is and they want someone, anyone, to cover their mortgage payment. These double listings SCREAM Motivated Seller! Now, not every single one of these is going to be an excellent Lease Option deal. But you know what? That's okay, there are plenty to choose from!

The critical part in selecting your Lease Option candidates, in an up market or a down market, is creating WIN-WIN-WIN situations. The seller must be satisfied with the deal, you must be satisfied and the end buyer must be satisfied. When investing in real estate this is what makes us successful. How does this work?

To create a WIN for someone we must meet their core need. A motivated seller's goal is to sell their house. Eventually they need that mortgage paid off and the deed transferred out of their name. If they are willing to rent the house as well as sell it, they are telling you that having their mortgage paid each month is more important right now than actually getting the house sold. If we can find a tenant buyer for them we are satisfying their core need of paying the mortgage each month and eventually selling the home. This is a WIN for the seller.

Our end buyer is looking for a home to own. Their current situation prevents them from getting a mortgage immediately but they plan on being able to get a mortgage soon. They want a home now. They don't want to wait to get their house. By allowing them to lease and then purchase the house we are meeting their core need. This gives our buyer a WIN.

Before we talk about what makes a WIN for us as an investor, let's talk a little more about mortgages for our end buyer. There has been a lot of news lately about sub-prime lending woes, how lenders with riskier loans are facing high rates of foreclosure and may be going bankrupt. As a result it is getting much harder for people with poor credit to obtain a mortgage. It is also getting harder for ANYONE to obtain a mortgage with 100% financing (i.e. no money out of the buyer's pocket). This may sound crazy, but this is actually a good thing for us when investing in real estate.

When investing in real estate by doing Lease Options it is harder for us to find quality tenant buyers when almost anyone who can fog a mirror can get a mortgage. Not only that but because it was so easy to get 100% financing most buyers save nothing and are unable or unwilling to pay much for an option fee. With the lending companies tightening their belts I expect we will see a growing population of QUALITY tenant buyers who are able to pay HIGHER option fees.

The flip side of this is that because lenders are tightening their belts your tenant buyers will need to work harder to restore their credit. It may take as much as 2 to 3 years for some tenant buyers to be able to qualify for mortgages instead of just 1 year as we had seen before.

The bottom line though is when investing in real estate by using Lease Options the difficulties of the mortgage lenders are just another reason why this down market is a GREAT time for us investors.

Now let's look at the last part of our WIN-WIN-WIN equation. The WIN for us, the investor. For us to WIN we need to make a profit. The profit comes both from the equity spread between your option price to the seller and the buyer's option price to you as well as any monthly cash flow in the rental payments. With Lease Options it pays to be creative. You'll find a lot more deals and be a lot more successful investing in real estate if you practice creativity in your structuring.

The most common motivated seller we encounter is the one who has little to no equity in his home. Too many real estate investors get calls from sellers only care about, "What's it worth?" and "What do you owe?" If the numbers are too close together, they say, "Sorry, can't help you." Click. They hang up the phone.

What if you pursue it a little further with a creative mind? A good question to always ask is "What are your monthly payments?" If the payments are lower than rental rates you may be able to make some monthly cash flow. Another good question to ask is, "How soon do you need to sell the house?" You may want to ask this question a couple of times while you are talking to them. You could be surprised to find that the number grows longer each time you ask. There aren't too many markets I can think of that stay down forever. Eventually the house should start appreciating again. If your option period to the seller is long enough you can capture appreciation to make your profit.

What about this, "Are you willing to bring money to closing to sell your house?" and if their monthly payment is higher than what you can rent the house for, "Are you willing to pay the difference between the rental amount and your monthly payment?" These two questions may seem brazen, but ask yourself, what have you got to lose? If the seller is fully leveraged on the house or their payment is higher than the rental rate you have nothing to lose, because if they aren't willing to make concessions then you can't help them!

Certainly some of us feel awkward in asking these questions, but trust me, if you ask this question 30 times, no matter how embarrassed you might feel at the beginning, you will start to feel much more comfortable by the end.

These are just a few creative questions you might come up with to try to find terms that will allow you, as the investor, to make a profit, a WIN for you. When you add all of three of these together, meeting the seller's need, meeting the buyer's need and you making a profit, you have created a WIN-WIN-WIN. This is what you MUST do to be successful when investing in real estate with Lease Options.

Do you see how much BETTER it can be to find deals in down markets? Motivated Sellers are **EVERYWHERE** and there are **FEWER** investors competing with you. Combining these two factors allows you to <u>choose</u> your deals with greater care. Always "Cherry Pick" your deals in a soft market. This is why experienced investors, who have been in both up markets and down markets, prefer the down markets. Soft markets can provide some of the best deals when investing in real estate.

You can learn more about Wendy Patton by going to www.WendyPatton.com. Sign up for her newsletter. If you don't own her book, *Lease Options and Subject To Deals*, you should order it while you are on her site. Wendy explains the subjects very well. It is on my list of mandatory reading in my coaching program.

Imagination is more important than knowledge.

For knowledge is limited to all we now know and understand, while imagination embraces the entire world, and all there ever will be to know and understand.

Albert Einstein

Chapter 13

Investment Seminars – Are They Worth it?

You can make a lot of money as a REI but you need education. If you want to take advantage of the red hot REI market, get as much education as fast as you can. This window of opportunity will not last forever.

Where do you get it? You can read books, enlist the help of mentors (a very wise choice), you can learn it on your own (time consuming and very expensive) and/or you can even attend seminars.

I have paid as much as $5,000 to attend weekend boot camps and I've spent as little as $0 to attend a one day event. I have never regretted paying the $5,000 because each boot camp had great take away information I applied to my businesses – even the ones which asked no fee have given me valuable information I later applied which resulted in creating wealth.

Author and Colorado Attorney Bill Bronchick believes seminars are beneficial, too (be sure to visit his website at www.LegalWiz.com). In an article entitled, *Are Real Estate Seminars Worth the Money?,* he writes:

If you read the news media, you'll see that there's a proliferation of new real estate gurus and seminars coming around to feed the endless demand for real estate these days. One event recently attracted over 30,000 people, with Donald Trump as the headliner (like he knows anything about buying a duplex?). So, how do you tell the good from the bad?

Well, first let me comment that I believe there is very little truly "bad" info out there. The difference is mainly price and quality of information. Here's some things you should consider when determining whether to invest in a real estate seminar:

1. Price. Be leery of very cheap or very expensive seminars. If the seminar is free, it's because the promoter wants to sell you something. It costs the promoter thousands of dollars to get people into a room, so expect a hard sales pitch. If the event is more than $1,000/day, you should also be concerned, unless the admission price includes follow-up training or substantial materials. I'm not saying that $5,000 boot camps are all bad, just make sure you're getting what you are paying for.

2. Class Size. If you are paying $5,000 for a boot camp, you should expect a small class size. If not, you are likely overpaying, since you won't be able to ask questions in a large group format.

3. Teaching Ability. Some gurus are knowledgeable, but are bad teachers. Make sure you have heard the speaker before or ask other people who have attended. There's nothing worse than paying to listen to a boring speaker or one that can't convey a topic in "plain English".

4. Value. Let's face it, some products are expensive because you believe they are worth more. Good marketing makes you believe "Bayer" is better than generic aspirin. Before you pay thousands of dollars for the "brand name" seminar, look into a cheaper version that isn't being marketed on T.V.

5. The "Pitch". Although as a rule, the cheaper the seminar, the greater the pitch for other products, some promoters do nothing but pitch, even at $5,000 boot camps. Ask other people who have attended the seminar to determine the teaching to-product-to pitch ratio.

There's nothing wrong with a promoter offering products and services at the less expensive seminars, but it's borderline insulting to have a non-stop sales pitch when you are paying $1,000 a day or more.

6. Refund Policy. Is there an open refund policy? This is very important. Ask up front. You should be very suspicious of any seminar that does not offer a refund policy.

7. Are You Serious About It? No matter how much or little you pay for a seminar, it's all up to you. No diet works without exercise and discipline and no real estate investing technique works without your hard work.

If you are just beginning, stay away from the expensive seminars until you are sure it is for you. Start with the $500 or less variety, let it sink in, then consider more advanced seminars when you have done a few deals.

Once you start making money, you should continue investing in your education, since your return will be well worth it. If you are the type who has been to seventeen seminars and haven't done a deal, consider this: "The Fault Lies Not Within the Stars But Within Ourselves."

Real estate investing will make you a lot of money if you learn the techniques and apply yourself. The bottom line is that education will help you avoid mistakes and learn new ideas. Read books, go to seminars and learn from other investors. Your best investment is in yourself.

I have attended several of his seminars, purchased his courses and happily own his books. I have even enjoyed one-on-one instruction from Bill. Sign up for Bill's newsletter by going to www.LegalWiz.com. If you will sign up you can get some valuable free information. I am on his list and you should be, too.

Our greatest battles are that with our own minds.

Jameson Frank

Chapter 14

Dare to Dream

One of my goals is to make dreamers of people. I want you to see the possibilities available and opportunities you can create. I want you to succeed in business and in your personal life. I want you to feel the exhilaration and rush of success.

Success means different things to different people. For some, it may mean having meaningful relationships. For others, it might mean making enough money so they can quit their day jobs. For still others, it may mean giving away a million dollars each year.

No matter how you personally define success, achieving it boils down to having a vision for tomorrow and a way to get there. The way to get there

is through setting goals, creating a definitive plan for achieving those goals, and then taking the necessary action, even when that means leaving your comfort zone and venturing into unfamiliar or uncomfortable territory.

Having the dream and knowing how to achieve it will be meaningless unless you do what you need to do to make it happen. Success means reaching your goals, not simply dreaming about them. The Greek Philosopher, Epictetus, said, "First say to yourself what you would be, and then do what you have to do."

To help you achieve success, I offer you a list of what I believe are the 10 most common reasons people fail to realize their dreams and advice on how to overcome them.

1. Get a clear vision of what you want to accomplish.

If you don't know what it is that you want, how will you know when you've arrived? The more distinct your dream becomes, and the better you articulate it, the faster you'll achieve it.

I want you to try an experiment. Put your feet flat on the floor with your back straight. Now, relax and close your eyes. I want you to picture success, whatever that is to you. I want you to explore the benefits and pleasure of that success. I want you to feel the exhilaration. Taste it. Smell it.

Success, however you viewed it in your dream, is true: it's your reality. That reality can be extended and enlarged upon. But without *seeing* what you now understand success to be, you'll never know what it is when you get there. In my book *My New Reality Journal*, [www.RealCashFlow.net and then "Products"] I encourage you to dream. I want you to have huge, expansive dreams. And I want you to clearly see where it is you're going.

2. Deal with the fear of failure.

Many people never really try to succeed because they fear failure. I'll let you in on a secret: it's okay to fail. In fact, I give you my permission to fail. I've learned some of my most important lessons through failure. It is true that some fear is

healthy. It is crucial to remember, however, to keep your fears and worries in perspective: if you let them overwhelm you, they may rob you of your dreams.

Successful entrepreneurs refuse to let worry, fear, and uncertainty hold them back from reaching their goals and realizing their potential. I want the same for you.

I challenge you to eliminate from your vocabulary words such as *if, can't, never,* or *won't.* Don't say, "If I'd had a better childhood, I could've_____" or, "I can't _____. I'm not smart or good looking enough."

Don't think things such as:
"I'm "such a jerk. How could I have said that?"
"I'm a loser. I'll never get anywhere."
"I'm so stupid. I should have learned this by now."

"I don't fit in. I don't belong with these people."
"I'll never be good enough. I'll never do it right."
"I'm permanently emotionally damaged. I'll never be okay."
"No one could love me. I'm not lovable."

Those kinds of words, and that kind of thinking, will almost certainly become self-fulfilling prophecies that will take you down a path away from where you want to go. Replace them with positive affirmations—restated in terms that reinforce positive behavior and a positive mindset.

Try these:
"This is going to be hard, but I know I can do it."
"I am as capable as anyone else."

"I have my own special talents and abilities."
"I'll stick with this as long as it takes."
"I'm a great person!"

These positive affirmations, especially when spoken frequently, will result in a new reality. You will see yourself in a new light. Just remember: whatever you think about yourself as it relates to success and achieving your dreams is true.

3. Possess determination.

We all face challenges that test our resolve. Often a challenge will stop us dead in our tracks. We hit a roadblock and our forward motion ceases. The goal, then, is to face such challenges without reservation and turn them into opportunities so we can continue forward.

Challenges can be viewed as an exciting ride. They can turn life into a treasure hunt or a grand adventure because you never know what you're going to find tomorrow. If I come up against a brick wall, I try to find the crack in the mortar or a hidden door I can open that will enable me to press on. Sometimes I have to go around the wall, and that's okay, too. It's still a journey worth taking.

I used to pray for challenges. I loved the opportunity to do what "they" said couldn't be done. If someone told me I couldn't, I had to prove him or her wrong. It was like saying to a dog, "sic 'em." I would charge out and do the undoable. (One day my wife asked me not to pray for any more challenges. She told me she didn't know if she could go along for the ride any longer!)

Determination is one thing that separates those who succeed from those who don't. Once you have a vision of where you want to go, resolve—*firmly*—to get there.

4. Make a plan of action.
To achieve a level of success, and hopefully significance, you need to create a precise plan detailing exactly what you must do to realize your dream. If you don't write it down, how will you know if you are making progress toward the goal? Be

sure, too, to set a timetable for completion of your tasks. Open-ended tasks seem always to be pushed to the rear of the priorities.

Break your objectives into daily activities and then manage those activities. You'll be surprised at how easy it is to complete a lot of work when you manage your time well. Don't let the phone, walk-in customers, or whatever "emergencies" may present themselves rule your life. Take charge. During certain hours, I refuse to take phone calls. I let them go to voice mail and return them when I arrive at the allotted time. I used to have a script on my voice mail that said, "Thanks for calling. I have several appointments today. I can return your call between 10 and 11 a.m. or 3 and 4 p.m. Please let me know when the best time for you would be." That simple script gave me back my life.

When you write your strategy, post it where you can easily see it and read it. You'll find that the more you look at it, the more likely you will be to accomplish the tasks you've set for yourself. Also, I find that it helps to deal with difficult things first: get anything distasteful or disagreeable over with or out of the way as soon as you can. That way, so you can enjoy the rest of the day. Also, do all you can without putting things off. Thomas Carlyle, the 9th Century Scottish essayist, wrote: "Men do less than they ought, unless they do all they can."

5. Make adjustments.

You will have to make adjustments in your life to focus on reaching the success you want. To make the time you will need, you may have to cut back on or even give up certain activities. The trick is to prioritize. You don't have to skip your daughter's basketball game or leave the bowling league or Friday night poker. But almost everyone has something he or she can spend less time on. Do you *have* to do the crossword or Sudoku *every* day? Try spending less time watching television, manicuring the lawn, or visiting friends on "MySpace."

Are you surrounded by people who can help you succeed? People can be a great help to you in reaching your goal, but they can also be a hindrance. Don't feel pressured by the friend who tells you not to worry about it, that you can do it tomorrow. Let people know that you are available only after you've done the things you need to do.

6. Eliminate negative thinking.

Everyone has some self-doubt. However, these two questions will help you. Each day ask yourself:

1. Did I give my best effort to today's activities?
2. Did I move closer to reaching my goals?

The answer to both, of course, should be "yes." If it isn't, though, don't kick yourself. Ask yourself why not, and do things differently tomorrow. Remember the positive affirmations discussed earlier.

Once again, it is important to look at the people in your life. You'll find it easier to do the things you need to do if people support your goals and respect your needs.

7. Embrace enthusiasm.

Be the day's cheerleader. All days are good; some are just better than others. You will find enthusiasm is contagious; give some to others. Show off! Tell people how happy you are to be pursuing your dream. And as you move closer to your goal, reward yourself with praise.

8. Take action and end procrastination.

I can't say this enough: you can have the best plan in the world, but if you don't take action on it you simply have a dream. Are you self-motivated, or do you need external motivation from someone else?

Self-motivated people are rewarded by their own achievements. Of course, all of us are pleased with ourselves for meeting goals. Some of us, though, are more motivated by positive feedback from others. This feedback may come in different forms. If your goal is financial, you may have friendly competitions with co-workers to see who gets the most contracts every week. If your goal is to be a poet, you may want to join a writers' group. You will find feedback and encouragement that will help you stay focused on your daily goals.

Determine which method of motivation works for you. Then take action.

9. Take personal responsibility.

You own your dream and your future. Of course, there may be setbacks and unforeseen circumstances, but you're going to treat those as opportunities, right?

It's easy to name all the things that rendered you incapable of reaching your goal, but it's a good deal more gratifying to tell how the same things didn't stop you, to describe the brilliance with which you met each challenge, or to explain how you were inspired to succeed. Successful people don't place blame or make excuses because they don't have to. Neither do you. There is almost nothing you can't plow through or work around.

10. Learn from your mistakes.

Mistakes. Everyone makes them. Successful people learn extremely valuable life lessons from their mistakes. Don't be ashamed of your blunders and, more importantly, don't be afraid to make more.

Imagine what the world would be like if scientists of the past, for example, failed to act for fear of making mistakes. Albert Einstein said, "The only sure way to avoid making mistakes is to have no new ideas."

So, envision your dream, determine what you will need to do to make it happen, and then do it. Remember that the things that slow us down can actually be used as stepping stones to greater successes. If you'll view the temporary setbacks as learning tools rather than negative life events, you are in a much better place to view the challenges with expectancy.

Identify what's holding you back. Then identify what you need to do to break through to success. If you work on changing your mindset to meet life's challenges, you'll reach your goals and realize your dreams.

Chapter 15

Hard Money Lenders

In declining markets, creative financing has helped thousands of real estate investors secure and close the purchase of property. Some creative options to consider are owner financing, HELOC loans, personal loans, credit cards and hard money lenders. The subject here is hard money loans. You can use hard money to help you complete flips, rehabs, construction, acquisition and development of land, and other non-stabilized commercial projects.

Hard money lenders are generally private lenders who will loan funds based on the value of a specific residential or commercial property. "Hard money" is a term that refers to the difficult nature of securing funding. They are loans that have high interest rates and a lower loan-to-value ratio. This is because there is no agency guaranteeing the loan will be paid so the loan is made against the value of real property used to collateralize the loan. If the borrower doesn't pay, the lender has a property he can sell quickly and get his investment back.

The basic difference in qualifying for hard money loans and traditional loans is that hard money loans are given by private lenders based on the value of the property, usually 60% to 70% of the market value, rather than on the credit worthiness or financial strength of the borrower, as in traditional bank lending. Hard money loans are not intended to be long term solutions. Rather, they should be used as short term bridge loans because the interest rates are usually higher than traditional bank loans. AN upside to hard money loans is that they are usually less costly than finding a full blown financial partner who will share in the profit even after you factor in the points charged by the lender. One "point" is equal to 1% of the loan value (if the lender charges 8 points, he is charging you 8% of the loan amount as a loan fee). Consider also these positive reasons to use hard money lenders:

1. You receive your funds in a matter of days, not months.

2. There is usually no risk to your personal credit.

3. If you develop relationships with private lenders you can be part of the "inner circle" of real estate investors who somehow find out about the best deals around and are building real wealth. (I have phone calls every week for

another "great" deal – so many in fact, I can't do them all).

There are times when there's not enough equity in a single property sufficient to meet the loan-to-value underwriting requirements of the lender. Since securing the property is the basis of making a hard money loan some hard money lenders will agree to "cross collateralize" on another property owned by the borrower. This is also referred to as a blanket mortgage. Cross collateralizing is more commonly used in commercial hard money loans. I have used this approach to secure short term financing. When the loan is paid off, the lender releases his interest in the property you ~~have~~ used for collateralization.

For residential purchases, you can, for example, buy a house in foreclosure by doing a short sale with a bank (fifty to sixty cents on the dollar), with a strategy to flip the house, and borrow the short term money needed to carry it for a BRIEF period of time until your buyer closes his loan. In a traditional setting you may have to wait 30 or 45 days to close a traditional loan, a time frame not acceptable to the bank from which you are doing your short sale. Since the hard money lender looks at the property, rather than normal underwriting guidelines, you can close your loan in a matter of days and the investor is still protected.

I was involved in a transaction which my bank assured me they would fund. The amount of the loan would have been a little more than $1,300,000. When time came to close the commercial loan, the bank backed out. To compound the problem I had the property sold to another party (this was a flip). To satisfy the terms of my purchase agreement I was forced to borrow $1,200,000 through a hard money lender for about two months. He charged me eight points ($96,000) and 14% interest. (The bank was going to loan to me at 7.5-8%).

Was this a good deal for me? Yes, because I received the $1,200,000 in about three days which saved the transaction. Additionally, I still made about $300,000. Some people would walk away from such a transaction because they don't want to pay those kinds of fees. However, when I placed in a corner I will look at the numbers, and if the deal still makes sense, I will proceed. The fee and interest rates are simply the cost of doing business.

Great buys abound in declining markets. Unfortunately cash shortages often go hand in hand with such a market making it difficult to fund these great buys. Hard money lenders fill a unique niche and they have their place. If used guardedly and carefully, they can be a benefit to your financial growth as you create wealth.

Please contact me if you are looking for hard money lenders or if you want to loan your money out. I may be able to put you in touch with reputable people who can help you. You can also do a Google search to locate hard money lenders. You will find them in your town, too. Ask real estate investors and mortgage brokers who they use. If you belong to an investing club you will find likely find a multitude of opportunities.

Chapter 16

Live Life to The Fullest

Have you ever felt like giving up? I mean, really give up! Are you are ready to give up on your marriage, dreams, or life itself? I have been there. I've felt the despair, failure, and helplessness as well as the feeling of being all alone. Those kinds of thoughts result when we believe the lies told to us. Lies such as, "I'm not good enough," "no one really loves me," "I have nothing to offer," and "I'm no good and I'll always be a failure." Because I've been there, I want to share with you a story of survival and accomplishment.

I was in Gold's Gym one morning 5 years ago when an attractive, petite, 5-foot-tall stranger, about my daughter's age, strolled by. New to the gym but with a look of experience, she was dressed for a workout at about 5:30 a.m.—pretty noteworthy in itself. She bore a raised, rectangular scar on her thigh: the telltale mark of a skin graft. I was struck by her determined and self-assured body language as she walked past me—although she wore a support on her left knee and a brace on a scarred and shriveled left arm and hand.

Over the course of the next few months, I watched her with interest. She was always upbeat, and always had something encouraging to say to others. I was very impressed by her tenacious workout: she was relentless despite her weaker left arm and hand. I was even more impressed that she seemed unaware that she might have any kind of limiting physical condition. Her attitude and demeanor were especially memorable because this is a place where many young women are concerned more with their makeup than their cardio.

A few weeks after I first saw her, when she and I were doing weight training, I was granted permission to ask a personal question. I asked about her arm and hand. She answered directly and honestly, and she has been my hero ever since.

Shannon Bart, my co-author and collaborator in a forthcoming book, is truly an amazing woman. Not only has she overcome challenges that would have stopped lesser people, she has excelled in spite of them. She's been an inspiration and source of incredible encouragement to many people. Her experiences, her education, her achievements, and her remarkable perspective on life make her uniquely qualified to contribute to this book and take the role of your coach and mentor. I think she will become your hero, too.

Here is her story:

Shannon was physically active in her youth. A talented gymnast, she pushed herself to compete and succeed, and as a freshman was a member of the gymnastics team at Arizona State University. Unfortunately, during a practice she tore her anterior cruciate ligament.

It was an injury that required surgery and marked the end of her gymnastics career. A hospital stay was followed by 6 weeks on crutches and in physical therapy. Although this could have been devastating, Shannon wasn't discouraged—she pressed on.

By the fall of 1997, Shannon was married and pregnant with her first child. But in October, 26 weeks into her pregnancy, she went into preterm labor for no apparent reason. Her doctor ordered strict best rest and tried to determine the nature of her condition.

Within a month, she was flown to the High Risk Pregnancy division of Columbia-Presbyterian St. Luke's Hospital in Denver, where her labor continued, her doctor still unable to uncover the underlying cause. Eventually, it was discovered that Shannon had a degenerative kidney disease. She would need a kidney transplant sometime within the next 5 years.

"Can I have more children?" she asked. Shannon and her husband, Sean, had talked about having three. "Maybe after you have a transplant," was the Doctor's bleak prognosis.

During the remainder of Shannon's pregnancy, she had to endure 11 weeks of steroid injections, strict bed rest, 2 amniocenteses, medication every 90 minutes and continual home monitoring. When that—and 30 hours of labor—was over, she delivered, by emergency Cesarean Section, a 3-pound, 10-ounce baby boy: Hunter. The little guy's heart stopped beating in the delivery room. Thankfully, he was resuscitated, but he had to stay in the hospital an additional 4 weeks. Hunter has grown into an energetic boy who wants to build houses, like his dad, and he is also the top speller in his class.

This sounds like a great success story already, doesn't it? But we're not through.

A mere 6 months later, Shannon's life, and that of her family, went spinning out of control. Shannon, Sean, and Hunter were on a road trip to Santa Fe, New Mexico to visit her mother. One morning, at about 5 a.m., Sean swerved their SUV to avoid a collision with a construction vehicle.

Their SUV flipped over. As the car rolled, Shannon's left arm and hand were thrust through the broken sun roof and skidded down the pavement beneath the overturned car. By the time the SUV landed upright, her arm and hand were crushed and stripped of flesh, muscle, and sinew. Sean pulled Shannon and Hunter from the car. He applied a tourniquet to her arm to stop the bleeding and flagged down a truck driver to call for help.

Shannon will always wear the scars of that accident. She has no idea how the surgeons put her arm back together: she calls it a medical and scientific marvel. She remembers asking the emergency room doctor, " ... are you going to give me something for the pain?" There was no pain yet, but she was sure there was going to be some very soon.

Healing came slowly: she endured another 2 weeks in an Albuquerque hospital and 7 more weeks in Albuquerque, healing. It took 12 months to return to a "normal" home lifestyle. With the help of Sean and family members, progress inched along at a snail's pace.

Even after four surgeries, a skin graft, a muscle graft, and a series of "cleaning outs," Shannon is missing about 3 inches of bone in her left arm. She is also missing nerve function and sensation, and she carries with her, wherever she goes, a metal plate and screws.

Instead of becoming bitter, or getting angry at God or the world about the misfortunes that have befallen her, Shannon has remained positive and grateful for what she does have: a family and friends who were always there for her.

Much to her credit and never-say-die attitude, she completed her Master's in Psychology while going through the horrors of rebuilding an arm.

"I love my arm," she tells me. "Even after the fourth surgery the physician was not sure I would keep it. If the graft had failed," she continues, "he would have had to amputate it. It is a daily reminder to me of how blessed I am to be alive. I have the opportunity to share my life with Sean and raise my son and grow old. My scars are a testament to who I am."

Shannon is my hero. Here's one reason: she didn't flinch when life threw her a curve ball. She isn't bashful or ashamed of those scars. She wants people to ask about them. She loves giving positive insight to people who need it. Does she want to revisit the challenge? Here's what she said: "I don't particularly want to do it again, but if God gave me the opportunity to do it all over without the accident I would tell him, 'no, thanks'". Since the accident, Shannon is a different person. I think she became a better one.

Eventually the Barts moved to Bend, Oregon, Shannon's home town, and found a new nephrologist. The first year back in Bend, she had five kidney infections. She underwent surgery, which seemed successful but 5 years later, her kidney began to fail.

More labs tests, medications, and doctor appointments came next. She had to consider dialysis and a kidney transplant. Shannon made the decision not to go on dialysis. She knew she had a health problem, but she never conceded she was sick—even when she was very ill. And, she didn't want to leave her son with memories of Mom in dialysis.

A seasoned surgery veteran, Shannon chose to have a kidney transplant before she needed dialysis. One day she told me, quite off the cuff, "Don, you won't see me for a few weeks. I'm going to Portland for a transplant." I didn't even know she had a problem, let alone know a serious one.

She described her choice to have surgery this way: "It's like you are walking down a train track, in a tunnel, in the wrong direction, and there's no way to get off. You know the train is going to hit you, you just don't know when."

The search began for a matching donor. Shannon found one in her own home: it was a great friend, Jeramie, who happened to be living with Shannon and Sean. The three of them went to a Portland transplant clinic. They spent 5 days in the hospital and an additional 4 weeks in recovery in a spacious hotel room nearby. Shannon's mother was there to care for Shannon and Jeramie. Shannon told me, "The whole thing would not have been such a blessed experience without all my family who visited, prayed, and supported us."

She calls this life threatening experience a "blessed experience." Many people I know might have found another way to describe it—and not in such positive terms. But this is one facet of Shannon that has earned her a place in my heart, and another reason she is my hero. In spite of the obstacles and challenges, she faces life and people positively with her chin up, treating life like a treasure hunt. She writes,

My recovery was an amazing experience. I felt healthy within 24 hours of the surgery. My labs were normal for the first time in almost ten years. I had no complications, no infection, no rejection, and a month off with no responsibility except to sleep, eat, read, and be well. I made a concerted effort to enjoy every minute of it and remember how happy I was. I have continued to enjoy great health and daily gratitude for being alive. I am a big proponent for living donor transplants and getting that transplant before people are at death's door.

And, characteristic of Shannon, she feels strongly that the story is not as much about her as it is about the people in her life who helped her through all her trials. She takes the spotlight off herself and places it on others. She believes this is their story. "It was easier," she wrote to me, "to be the patient than to be the ones in the hospital waiting room. I wouldn't have traded spots with them for anything in the world."

She has tremendous respect and love for her husband, Sean. She recently confided to me, "... my husband, Sean, has never wavered in his love or support. I am not the woman he married. I have changed physically and personally and he has never looked at me differently than the day we got married. Okay, maybe differently—but not in a lesser fashion. He is my hero for so many reasons."

This wonderful, beautiful woman I've described to you is truly in a unique position to serve as your role model. It's my hope that you can get a new positive picture of what life can be. If you think there is nothing to live for, think again. If you think God has turned His back on you, He hasn't. If you believe you've nothing for which to live, you're wrong.

God has a plan for your life. A good plan, too. But as long as you're focused on your own "problems" you won't be able to see what that plan is and enjoy the life God has for you. Here's what I want you to do:

Step One: Whenever you are at your "rope's end," think in on the good things. Even when life seems bleak, there is always some good on which you can identify.

Step Two: When you don't know what else to do, focus on others. One of the basic flaws in our psychological culture is its focus and obsession with "self." Here's the truth: if you can learn to be concerned with the needs of others, you won't have the time or energy to think about your own "problems."

Step Three: If you come face to face with despair, learn to give. After you've learned to focus on the needs of others, learn how to give to others. Freely give your time, money, and services to good causes.

Step Four: Take personal responsibility for your actions. If you blame others for your position is life, those whom you blame are controlling you and you cannot move forward. If you've made poor choices, say so and break the vicious cycle and go on to greatness. It is your choice.

Regardless of where you are in life, or the challenges you face, there are millions of people who would probably trade places with you. Shannon has faced many more obstacles than you or I will ever have to face. Let her be your hero and role model. If she can prosper in spite of her challenges (or "opportunities" as she would describe them), so can you.

It is now up to you. The only question that remains is, will you become an achiever? You can! Will you?

My challenge to you is to go for it! Live life to the fullest and don't believe the lies, believe only the truth: You are bright enough, smart enough, good looking enough, and all the other positive words you can imagine.

Be sure to include God in your life. A relationship with Him will help bring the whole picture into focus and help make the impossible possible. Know that God loves you and has a plan for your life.

Adapted from Don Loyd's book, *Creating Wealth for Women*)

Chapter 17

How to Set Goals

How to set goals? Like all things, its actually quite simple – once you've done the ground work, which is:

- Get the 'Big-Picture' first, and always keep your eye on it.

- Work out what you REALLY want, not what you think you want.

- Work out what you can realistically do and achieve.

These are the foundations or the 'rocks' of your goal setting process. They set the direction for your goals, so it's really important to put the time into working them out properly. And they are unique to you, which is why only you can do it.

Once you've worked this out, you can **prioritize** and set your goals! You've probably heard of SMART Goals, well ours are SMARTer, which guarantees your goals contain all the necessary components to maximize your goal setting success.

Goal setting is of course an on-going and dynamic process. Your priorities and therefore your goals will change from time to time (for example if you start a family) and when this happens, it's important to sit down and go through the goal setting process again.

Also as you grow older and mature, your motivators and drivers will change so on-going review is necessary to make sure your goals are still relevant to you.

What you want when you're 20 will not be the same as what you want when you are 40. But armed with these skills, it is a tool for life – no matter what stage you're at or how old you are.

Keep reading to find out more on how to set goals.

Get the 'Big-Picture' first

The first and most important step in how to set goals - what is YOUR 'Big-Picture'?

This is one of those philosophical questions that go in the same boat as "What's the meaning of life?" and "Why are we here?", and you may never be able to truly answer it for yourself.

But if you want to try to define it, your 'big-picture' is your one guiding principle, your shining light, that forms the basis for all your decisions and actions.

If you were a company, your 'big-picture' would be the Vision or Mission Statement.

So, it is a statement outlining an idealized description of your life's outcome. It will inspire you and create your target. It can apply to different parts of your life – your family, your career – and it is the end target that you want to achieve, and where your goals need to take you.

To help you work out exactly what your 'big-picture' is, think about your tomb-stone. Macabre I know, but your tomb stone is a concise summary of your life – what you have achieved, and how people remember you.

How do you want to be remembered?

Of course, you may want to be remembered in several ways – as a career woman, family man, skilled professional – there are many aspects of your life that you need to consider. Too much focus on one aspect of your life could leave you feeling empty in another.

The classic example here is people who focus too much on their career driven by 'empty' goals of power, ambition and making money, only to neglect their family. Most of these people when on their death bed wish that they had spent more time on the 'important' things in life – an indication that they didn't get a handle on their personal 'big-picture'.

It's a question of balance, and you're the only one who knows the perfect balance for you.

You may not be able to put your 'big-picture' in words, but try to visualize what your life would be like if it was perfect in every way - this is your 'big-picture', and your goal setting needs to reflect it.

This is critical for how to set goals.

So what do you really WANT?

Now that you have an eye on your 'big-picture', what do you REALLY want?

Remember that goals must be personal and meaningful, otherwise you'll have no reason to achieve them. So you need to work out what YOU really want, not what other people think you want. This is the key to how to set goals.

The best way to work out what you really want is to brainstorm your thoughts to come up with a wish-list for each of your relevant life aspects. This is the chance for you to let loose by picturing your perfect life, and putting down in writing what that perfect life would look like.

Mind-Mapping is a great way to get to the heart of all your dreams and desires - just what you need for how to set goals.

What's a Mind Map? It's an attempt to de-jumble your mind into some logic, and allows you to set the scene for what you really want.

The importance to goal setting is that by using the Mind Mapping concept, you can cover all of your life aspects on the same piece of paper instead of traditional brainstorming where you'll end up with a separate list for each life aspect you want to consider.

And since life aspects are heavily connected, using a Mind Map gives you a considerable advantage for how to set goals.

So what can you really ACHIEVE?

The Mind Mapping process will give you a really good idea of what you really want, but in how to set goals you also need to know what can you really achieve?

Well, hypothetically, you can achieve anything you want to – but that's not always the case. Resources, natural skill and ability, time – these all factor into whether we can achieve something or not.

The aim of goal setting is to set achievable goals, even if that means taking a larger goal or dream and breaking it down into bite-size chunks.

A personal SWOT analysis is a great way to work this out – it's a detailed look at you and your life and will help you identify the most beneficial goals worth pursuing right now based on your current situation, and to identify goals that will help you prepare for the future.

For the purposes of goal setting, it is useful to perform a SWOT analysis on each life aspect as it will help you identify where you need to improve, and therefore help you set goals to make these improvements.

More importantly though, the SWOT analysis allows you to identify your internal strengths that you can capitalize on to sieze your opportunities and thwart any external threats.

A template for your personal SWOT analysis is available in the ToolBOX. Print out a separate page for each life aspect you want to analyze, and summarise the results on the SWOT Summary page, also available in the ToolBOX.

And find out more on how to do a SWOT analysis under the "Life Skills" tab on the NavBar under Decision Making and Problem Solving.

Prioritize and Synergize

So you should now have your 'big-picture' [as a tombstone inscription], a wish-list of what you really want [from your Mind Map] and an analysis of what you can actually achieve [from your personal SWOT analysis].

It's now time to pick the first goal or couple of goals to focus on.

Why only 1 or 2? Goal setting is a skill, and like all skills, how to set goals takes time and practice to become proficient at it. So start with a single, easy goal or two to practice on. Once you've achieved this one (or made some progress towards it), you'll feel motivated to try the process on some harder goals and confident in applying the process.

In the meantime, don't throw out all the work you've done – just because you're not actively pursuing a goal doesn't make it any less important. Just put these on the backburner until you've got some successful goal setting under your belt.

How to chose which goal? Well you need to consider:

- How important the goal is to you – prioritize! Starting on high priority goals will keep you more focused and motivated to achieve, than goals that are just considered 'nice to do'.

- The type of goal – 'habit' changing goals are often short-term goals and may therefore be easier to achieve. 'Skill' goals can have quite a clear path and may therefore appear easy, but beware that 'skill' type goals can take a long time to achieve so its important that they have lots of milestones to make the process manageable. 'Outcome' goals can be easy or hard, long or short, depending on exactly what they are.

- How comfortable are you that you know HOW to achieve the goal – for example, achieving optimum health and fitness may be a Must-Do goal for you and there is heaps of information and guidance on how it can be done, so that would be a good goal to chose as a starting point rather than something like achieving world domination!

- Make the most of goal synergy – some goals have benefits in several life aspects. How to set goals that synergize? Riding your bike to work for a 'fitness' goal will also help the planet and your hip pocket. Kill as many birds as you can with the one stone for maximum goal setting success!

In a nutshell, prioritize and synergize!

Make your Goal SMART

Once you have a set of personal goals that are meaningful to you and will ultimately help you achieve your 'big-picture', all you need to do is develop your chosen goals and make sure they're SMART or SMARTer.

How to set goals that are SMART? All you have to do is document the goal in the following easy to follow format:

S	Specific	Complete the sentence "My goal is to .... ". This makes it specific. And by linking this to a life aspect and a Big-Picture statement, you also make this goal give you direction, motivation and focus towards what you really want.
M	Measurable	Identify a measurement system for your goal. As well as noting HOW you are going to measure your goal (whether it be a real unit of measurement or a ranking type system), also note your 'starting' measurement.
A	Action-oriented	Identify the steps required to complete your goal – these are the actions that will form the basis of your personal Action Plan [see the 'how to achieve a goal' tab on the Navbar].
R	Reasoned and realistic	Complete the sentence "I want to achieve this goal because .... ". This statement will be the on-going motivation to drive you to achieve this goal. Ask yourself whether this goal is realistic or not.
T	Time-bound	Identify how long it will take to complete each step on your action plan and set yourself a deadline.
E	Ethical, Exciting and Enjoyable	Is your goal ethical, enjoyable and exciting?
R	Resourced	Identify the resources (time, money, support, information, etc) needed for you to achieve your goal. Make sure you include any sacrifices you have to make in here too.

When you've documented your goal, read it through – this is the crux of how to set goals and if you don't believe what you've written, now is the time to go back and look at why.

You need to commit to what you have written, so ask yourself:

- Am I really committed to undertaking the actions I have prepared?

- Am I really committed to achieving the action items within the timeframe I have set?

- Am I convinced that this is what I really want?

- Am I excited about the outcome from this goal?

- Am I prepared to allocate the resources and make the sacrifices I have identified?

- Am I actually going to do it?

If you answered "YES" to all of these questions, great! Continue to the 'How to achieve goals' tab on the NavBar.

If you aren't sure or had some "No's" in there, then you need to go back and look at 'why' - there is no point continuing if the goal you've developed and documented has a flaw in it.

A template for documenting how to set goals that are SMART is available in the ToolBOX. There are 2 versions available for you to chose from, depending on how much information you want to include.

The 'My SMARTER Goals' template allows you to write several goals on the one page, where as the 'SMARTER Goal' template is for a single goal only, but allows you to include more detail.

By Sam Sanders, www.achieve-goal-setting-success.com
Used with permission
Visit Sam Sanders success webpage at
www.achieve-goal-setting-success.com

Chapter 18

How to Achieve Goals

By Sam Sanders, www.achieve-goal-setting-success.com
Used with permission

How to achieve goals?
Well, here are the steps for how to achieve goals:

- Step 1: You need a SMART Goal

- Step 2: You need an Action Plan for your goal

- Step 3: You need to TAKE ACTION

- Step 4: Review your progress against your goal – regularly!

- Step 5: Reward yourself for you successes.

So, first of all you need a fully developed SMART goal – you need a Goal that is Specific, Measurable,

Action-orientated, Reasoned, Realistic, Time-bound, Ethical, Exciting, Enjoyable and Resourced. See the "How to set goals" tab on the Navbar if you're not sure about how to make your goals SMART.

Once you have a SMART Goal, you need to take action. Think of your goals as your target destination – so the Action Plan is how you get there! This is the FIRE part of READY-AIM-FIRE.

So often people produce fantastic SMARTER goals that just sit on the shelf and of course, nothing happens to make these goals become a success. Goals won't magically happen just because you've written them down.

You still need to MAKE them happen, by taking action – FIRE! Keep reading to find out more on how to achieve goals.

Developing your Action Plan

A SMART Goal will have actions in the "A" part - this is how to achieve goals. Depending on your goal, these Action Items may be detailed enough for you to work through your goal.

Not sure? Well, ask yourself the question: "If these Action Items were my only set of instructions to achieve this goal, would I be able to achieve it?". If your answer is "YES", well great!

If your answer is "No", take the time now to fully develop your Action Plan by expanding on these Action Items so that you have a truly actionable plan to achieve your goals.

Simply do this by taking each Action Item from your completed SMARTER Goal template and list the steps needed for each action item – include as much detail as necessary including the "What", "When", "Where", "Why", "How" and "Who".

To help you prepare a detailed Action Plan, you may opt to use the Action Plan template available in the ToolBOX.

The KEY to Achieving Goals

The key to how to achieve goals is taking action. The key to getting action on your goals is to integrate the goal's action

plan into your day-to-day routine and tasks, and that's where it's important to have 'Planners' and 'Schedules'.

It's all about getting yourself organized! Have a look at the Planning and Organization Skills under the 'Life Skills' tab on the NavBar.

'Planners' are specifically for listing the action items or steps for how to achieve goals, and 'schedules' are used to see how the action plan should pan out over the program and to identify any conflicts in resourcing.

'Schedules' will give you a visual representation of effort and how to achieve goals. For example, if you prepare a yearly schedule, and it shows lots of activity in the first 3 months but not much after that, you either have a short term goal only with lots of mini-tasks or you've crammed too much into the early stages of your Action Plan – be realistic about how much you can take on at any one time.

'Planners' are used to incorporate your goal setting actions and day-to-day activities into the one memory-jogging list, and are the cornerstone of how to achieve goals.

Depending on the goal, Planners could be a daily plan, weekly, monthly, quarterly, yearly or any-other suitable time frame. For example, a healthy eating and exercise plan may have daily actions if you want to be very specific about your activities, where as a budgeting plan may only have weekly actions, and career development goals may be even longer.

It doesn't matter which timeframe you adopt – chose the one that best suits the level of control you want to have over the Action Plan. Daily action plans will have the highest level of control.

Find a system that works for you. The key here is to be organized – 'Owls' are going to love this, but if you're an 'Eagle' or a 'Peacock', you may find it hard to be disciplined enough to stay organized, but it pays off as you start to achieve your goal. You'll also be more productive and efficient in your day-to-day activities if you're better organized.

'Doves', you'll be great with the organization part of this step, but make sure you put your personal goals high on your priority list and don't fall into the trap of looking after everyone else first.

Templates for several different time-scaled schedules and planners are available in the ToolBOX [on Sam's website].

Why you need to monitor and review your Action Plan and Goals

Reviewing goals and your progress towards your goals is a critical part of how to achieve goals.

Goal setting is a dynamic process. Over the long term, your vision will change - goals you had when you were a kid were different to those as a teenager because your needs change, and so does your situation in life.

You may recall (or maybe not if you are in the US) the Australian TV advertisement that surmises success in your 20's is making out, success in your 30's is taking a break, success in your 40's is making money, success in your 50's is making more money, success in your 60's is taking a break and success in your 70's is making out.

So, it is good practice to go through the whole goal setting process (yes, go through the whole thing again) every year or 2 and at least every 5 years, or if your life takes a sudden change in direction – for example, starting a family – to ensure you are always chasing the right 'Big-Picture'.

You can monitor the current 'truth' in your goal-setting journey by periodically reviewing your Mind Map and SWOT analysis – the important thing to ask yourself in this case is "does this still apply to me or has it changed?"

By doing this you will pick up any early signs that your life is wanting to take a different journey to the one you've planned, and this is perfectly normal and in fact expected as your life progresses. The key thing is not to see a change in plans as a failure, it's just a refocusing exercise.

Even short term goals need to be flexible enough to accommodate things that are out of your control (for example, other priorities on your time), or even things that are in your control but you just underestimated during your goal setting exercise (for example, underestimating how long it takes to quit a habit).

Don't worry if your goals don't go exactly according to your action plan, as long as you're making progress in the right direction and make sure you update your action plan to suit so that it is still meaningful to you for achieving your goal. Remember the SMARTER components of your goal always need to apply.

What do you do once you've achieved a goal?

First of all, congratulate yourself on a job well done. It doesn't matter how big or small your goal was, completion of a goal represents a step in the right direction towards your life success!

Reward yourself for your efforts with an appropriate treat [not a huge slice of chocolate cake if your goal was to lose weight!] – it sometimes helps to set this reward when setting the initial goal to help with motivation along the way, of course completion of the reward gives you a real buzz which is often a reward in itself!

But don't stop here - set a new goal. Perhaps this was just a mini goal you've achieved - start the next mini-goal towards your milestone. Or have you achieved a milestone? In which case, go back through your list of goals and develop the next goal to start on. Does your available effort and resources allow you to work on another couple of goals?

Goal setting is a life-long process – your goals will change along the way, but you should always have some. As you become more experienced in the goal setting process, you will feel a lot more confident in setting and working towards multiple and more complex goals. Build on your experiences both good and bad and be the best that you can be and SUCCEED!

How to achieve goals? Remember, it's all about you and it's all up to you – you're the only one who can set and achieve your goals.

Visit Sam Sanders success webpage at
www.achieve-goal-setting-success.com

Chapter 19

Quick Success Secrets

By Sam Sanders www.achieve-goal-setting-success.com
Used with permission

Here are some quick success secrets because we know you're busy and don't want to spend your time reading through pages and pages of information. So in a nut-shell, here are the secrets of success.

Know what 'success' means to you

- What does 'success' mean to you – in your career, personal life and relationships. What do you REALLY want?

- Know that your idea of success needs to be personal and meaningful to YOU.

- Know that being successful brings satisfaction and contributes to your overall happiness.

- Understand that 'success' isn't measured in dollars, it's measured in how satisfied you feel.

- Understand that happiness is NOT achieved from material possessions, hence understand the fallacy of western society's culture of consumerism [read the warning on consumerism to find out why].

- Visualize your 'success' so that you can strive towards it.

Research has shown that 'happiness' [not success] is achieved from having meaningful and loving relationships and enough money (about $100,000 pa income). Not having enough money and the 'stress' of having too much money both contribute to unhappiness, as do bad and unhealthy relationships.

Imitate success

- Visualize your 'success' so that you can strive towards it.

- Identify a suitable 'successful' role model and observe and emulate how they dress, behave and act. Learn their success secrets. BUT – be yourself too!

- Learn the skills required for success – communication and professionalism.

- Dress for success – dress to the standards of the job you want [taking appropriate work uniform requirements into account of course!]. Dress like your boss, if your goal is to one day do his job.

- Always be ethical, honest and act with integrity.

- Use your initiative and always be on the lookout for opportunities.

It's all about YOU!

- You are unique and will have a unique set of dreams and desires – follow these, and not anyone else's.

- Your personality is also unique to you, and will influence your idea of success and how you achieve it.

- Understand how your personality influences your success and use this to help you achieve.

- Know your personal strengths and weaknesses, and use this knowledge to your advantage. These are your personal success secrets.

- Always be honest with yourself and your abilities.

Get the right attitude

- 90% of success is about your personal attitude.

- Know that positive attitude is a powerful force in achievement.

- Know that a negative attitude is destructive to your happiness and your ability to succeed.

- Know that your attitude and your mood is governed by you alone and your thoughts – no-one else can control your attitude.

- Get a positive attitude by exposing your self to positive people, images and media – and avoid negative influences.

- Use visualization and positive reinforcement to get the message.

Studies have shown that people you expose themselves to negative ideas, thoughts and environments are more negative, depressed and unmotivated [and therefore less likely to succeed] than people you expose themselves to mostly positive ideas, thoughts and environments.

The media is a major player in providing a negative environment – so don't watch too much TV!

Set Goals – regularly

- It is well known that people with goals succeed, and people who succeed have goals.

- Goals MUST be meaningful and personal – otherwise you won't be inspired to achieve them.

- Goals give you something to aim for.

- Goals help you focus your time and energy on achieving you're the right things.

- Goals give you motivation – because goals are MEANINGFUL and personal to you, you'll look forward to achieving them.

- Goals help you break up seemingly impossible dreams into manageable, bite-sized pieces.

- Your Goals will change as your life progresses. Understand that goal setting is a dynamic and never-ending process if you want your life to be a success.

Take Action

- There is no point having READY and AIM if there is no FIRE.

- Know that no-one has achieved success by sitting on their butt [excuse the language].

- Know that to achieve success you must TAKE ACTION.

- For action you need 'Motivation', which comes from having goals and the right attitude.

- Use Action Plans with deadlines to guide you. If goals are your target destination, action plans are your road map to success.

Understand People

- Understand that 90% of what you do will involve other people, and that achieving your personal success will also involve other people.

- Understand that you will achieve more by fostering good relationships with other people and you will if you don't.

- Just as you are unique and have personal likes and dislikes, so do other people.

- Understand yourself, and how other people react to you. Use this understanding to your advantage, so you can better foster good relationships.

- It's not always about you!

- This is the concept of 'Emotional Intelligence' (EQ) and is one of life's poorly understood success secrets. Understand that people with a high EQ are more likely to succeed than people with a low EQ.

Manage your career

- Understand that your 'career' occupies more of your waking hours than anything else. Make this time count and enjoy it!

- Understand that being a 'stay-at-home' mum or dad is a career – a very rewarding one.

- Understand that you can achieve happiness through job satisfaction and success.

- Embrace the saying "If you truly love your job, you'll never work a day in your life."

- Embrace the concept of continuous improvement – aim to be the best in your field.

- Be proactive in chasing challenging job opportunities – use initiative and drive.

Manage yourself – get life skills

As well as the specific skills you need for your career, particular 'self-management' skills will help you be successful in all aspects of life:

- Time management – know how to make the most of the time you have, whether at work or in your own personal time

- Planning and organization – understand that being organized will help you achieve your goals.

- Decision making and problem solving – know how to make the right decisions and solve problems.

- People skills – Understand that 90% of what you do will involve other people, and that achieving your personal success will also involve other people

- Self-Motivation and Attitude – understand that YOU are the only person who can make your life happen the way you want it to and that your attitude and motivation are critical for action.

Manage your finances

- Understand that a certain amount of money is necessary – too little will cause stress and having too much also has this affect. .

- Know how much money you REALLY need. The endless pursuit of more money for no reason will ultimately end in failure and your unhappiness.

- Understand that financial management is just a skill – it's not hard and there are no magic tricks.

- Maintain a healthy awareness of your finances – know what you earn and owe.

- Budget, and make the most of what you've got.

- Develop a savings plan, for that rainy day.

- Do your best to reduce, or at least consolidate, personal debt. Don't over-rely on credit cards.

- Scrutinize expenditure and prioritise your spending – must spend | should spend | nice to spend.

- Invest for your future and plan for retirement.

- Understand that to make money, you need to spend money – but do this wisely.

- Understand that high return investments are ALWAYS high risk, or high input. If an investment sound too good to be true, it is!

- Use tax laws to your advantage, but NEVER break them – the Tax Man will catch up with you eventually. Get the advice from your accountant if in doubt.

- Beware of scams and 'get rich quick' schemes. Beware of any scheme from Nigeria – the scam capital of the world!

- Take care of your big assets – your house, and to a lesser extent, your car.

- Protect your valuables with insurance – your health, your income, your life and your assets.

Look after your health

- Remember that you only have one body - so look after it!

- Realize that first impressions matter. You will project a more successful image if you appear to take good care of your own health.

- Know your health is the combined result of diet, exercise, sleep, stress and lifestyle – achieving the right balance is the key.

- Understand that taking care of your health is not vanity.

Have meaningful relationships

- No-one on their death-bed wished that they had spent less time with their family – don't let this be your dieing wish.

- Understand that having meaningful relationships with your partner, kids and extended family has a bigger impact on your happiness than material success.

- Similarly, good friendships are an important factor in having a happy life.

- Surround yourself with family and friends that bring out the best in you.

- Teach your kids these success secrets too, so they can be the best they can be! And most importantly...

The grand-daddy of all success secrets: DO WHAT MAKES YOU HAPPY.

Visit Sam Sanders success webpage at www.achieve-goal-setting-success.com

It all begins with a dream.

A dream is like a seed that when

watered and nourished

grows into a grand

experience or noble cause.

If you want to see tomorrow,

dream.

A dream is a glimpse into the

future.

Don Loyd

Don Loyd's Real Estate Investing Quick Start *Action* Plan

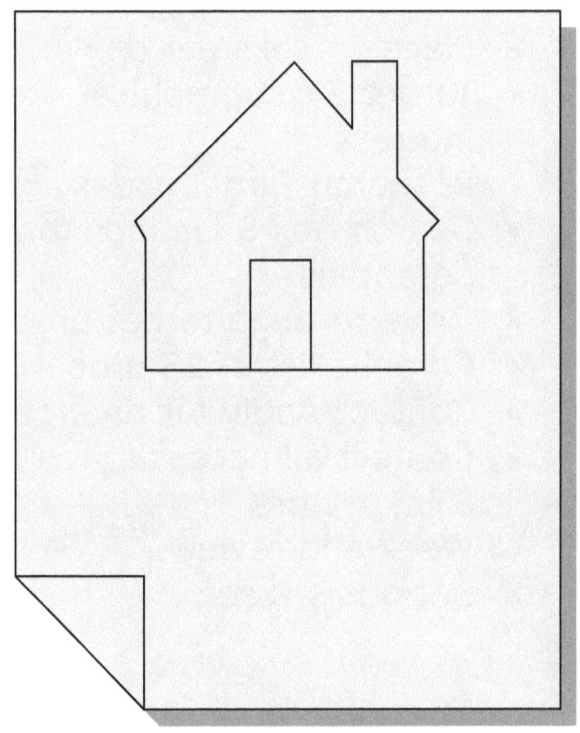

My Daily Goal:_____

My Monthly Goal: _____

My Yearly Goal: _____

Don Loyd's

Quick-Start *Action* Plan

Weekly Plan of *Action*

This Week's *Actions*:

- Place ___ calls per day
- Target 2 Geographical Areas of interest
- Research Target Areas
- Search Ads & Listings for potentials
- Drive through target areas
- Compile list of 25 properties
- Contact/Apply for finances
- Contact all necessary contractors & inspectors
- Week end review
- Set goals *Week 2*

Appts.
Property Calls
Target Area Research
Consultant &Contractor Calls
Ad Searches
Ad Placements
Drive-bys
Other
Evaluate

How many activities will you engage on a daily basis? Plan out your day the night before.

Today's *Action* Objective

Today's Priority

_____

_____

_____

_____

Weekly Objective

_____

_____

Daily *Action* Tracker

_____
(Day)
_____
(Date)

To Do Today
(check jobs that *must* be done *today*)

☐ _____

_____

☐ _____

_____

☐ _____

_____

☐ _____

_____

☐ _____

_____

☐ _____

_____

Tomorrow's Follow-Up *Actions*:

_____

_____

_____

_____

_____

_____

_____

_____

_____

_____

_____

_____

_____

_____

_____

_____

_____

_____

_____

_____

_____

Don Loyd's
Quick-Start *Action* Plan
Action Calls Log

Name _____

Contact/Ad Source _____

Property Address

_____

Date of Contact _____

Discussed _____

_____

_____

_____

Follow-Up *Action*

_____

_____

_____

Rate Property Potential

☐Excellent (priority target) ☐Fair (worth

considering) ☐Poor (no chance)

Don Loyd's
Quick-Start *Action* Plan

Ready for *Action*–
Placed Ads Log

Calls
Received
————

Publication/Location of Ad

_____

Contact Person

_____

Date Placed _____

Ad Copy (write or staple ad here)

_____

_____

_____

How worthwhile is advertising *Action?*

□ Great Response! Keep placing Ads. □ Mediocre
Response; Start reconsidering.
□ Minimal at Best; Try something else.

Don Loyd's
Quick-Start *Action* **Plan**

Search *Action* –

Source of Information
□Newspaper
□Real Estate Catalog/Agent
□Foreclosure list
□Drive-by
□Cold Call
□Online
□Other

Type of Property
Currently offered as
□Rental
□Rent-to-
 Own
□FSBO
□For Sale (R.E.Agent)
□Foreclosure
□Other

Investment Potential
□Low

□Very Good

□Mid-level

Don Loyd's
Search *Action*
Potential Property Log

Property Address:	**Size of Building:**

Exterior Inspection:(note apparent condition of the following)

Windows & Trim
Driveway
Siding
Cleanliness
Paint
Septic   Public or Private
Yard
Neighborhood
Roof

'Bones':(note structural condition)

- Rotten   - Some visible rot
- Good   - Excellent
- Needs Inspection

Needs Prof. Inspection:

- Plumbing   - Electrical
- Mold   - Water
- Heating   - Other

Interior Inspection:(note apparent condition of the following)

Windows
Bathroom
Fixtures?
Trim

Kitchen
Fixtures & Appliances?
Walls
Attic
Paint?
Tile?

Basement
Floors
Heating System

Overall cleanliness
Visible mold growth?

Needs Prof. Inspection:

- Plumbing
- Mold
- Heating
- Electrical
- Water
- Other

Week of *Action* in Review

Estimate Your Rate of Task Completion:
(100%, 90, 85...)

How happy are you with your progress?
☐Thrilled   ☐Satisfied

What I Enjoyed the Most:

Looking Ahead...

Place

Ads Next Week

Find

Property Ads Next Week

Next Target Area:

To Do Next Week: (include follow-up actions from weekly plan and uncompleted tasks to carry over from this week)

Don Loyd's RICH SYSTEM ™

R – *Return?* – How much wealth does this property create for me today? This is not appreciation or how much you can sell it for next year.

I – *Investment?* – How much money out of my pocket will this take? Normally, I want to put in as little money as necessary.

C – *Cash Back?* – If I put money in, when do I get it back?
The goal is to get your money back as soon as possible so you can do more investing.

H – *Holding Income?* – Does the property have positive cash flow? You want to avoid negative cash flow. It can put you out of business.

Goal setting helps you:

- Work out what you really want – this is personal. You're the only one who knows what you really want, and it's often not what you think.

- Work out a plan of attack to help you achieve what you really want – there is no point having a great goal if you don't know how to get there.

- Give you the motivation to put your plan into action – since your goals will be personal and meaningful to you and based on what you really want, you will be motivated to achieve it. But you also need the right 'can-do' attitude!

Keep track of where you are going by helping you focus on the 'big picture', to ensure you don't lose your direction – it's easy to get distracted by life's little obstacles, so goal setting will help you focus your time and energy in

Sam Sanders

The price of success is hard work,

dedication to the job at hand,

and the determination that

whether we win or lose,

we have applied the best of

ourselves to the task at hand.

Vince Lombardi

www.ingramcontent.com/pod-product-compliance
Lightning Source LLC
Chambersburg PA
CBHW022003170526
45157CB00003B/1128